SACRED WEALTH

SACRED WEALTH

ACTIVATING YOUR INNER ABUNDANCE

△ ALY WILKINS △

ALY WILKINS
ENERGY HEALING + MENTORSHIP

SACRED WEALTH

Cover Design by Lori Menna at Cosmic Collage
ISBN-13 : 978-0-578-80184-1

For more, visit www.AlyWilkins.Me or e-mail AlyWilkinsAbundance@gmail.com.

DISCLAIMER

This book is for general informational purposes only. It is not intended as a substitute for the medical advice of physicians. The reader should regularly consult a physician in matters relating to his/her health and particularly with respect to any symptoms that may require diagnosis or medical attention. Although the Author has made every effort to ensure that the information in this book was correct at press time, the Author does not assume and hereby disclaim any liability to any party for any loss, damage, or disruption caused by this book. The Author and/or distributors are not responsible for any adverse effects resulting from the use of the suggestions outlined in this program. Any use of this information is at your own risk. The information contained within this book is strictly for spiritual educational purposes. If you wish to apply ideas contained in this book, you are taking full responsibility for your actions.

THANK YOU.

A special thank you to all of the Light Leaders who have come before me. Thank you for guiding the way and paving the path. I deeply honor and appreciate your commitment to the new paradigm of Love.

A special thank you to the Reader, for your commitment to becoming your Highest Self and honoring the Divinity within.

Always remember who you are.

More From Aly:

40 Day Sacred Wealth Ritual
A guided 40-day abundance ritual to attract more abundance into your life, utilizing the loving forces of Divinity while simultaneously re-programming your conditioning around abundance. This is a highly rated product and Aly's signature program. Learn more and get access at www.AlyWilkins.Me.

Akashic Record Readings
Visit www.AlyWilkins.Me to book your Akashic Record session with Aly. See the website for reviews and more information.

1:1 Spiritual Mentorship
E-mail AlyWilkinsAbundance@gmail.com to book your mentorship session with Aly. See www.AlyWilkins.Me for reviews and current offerings.

Group Retreats + Individual Retreats
See www.AlyWilkins.Me for up-to-date retreat offerings or e-mail AlyWilkinsAbundance@gmail.com if you'd like to book a private or group retreat.

DoTerra Oils
You can purchase DoTerra oils from Aly at www.AlyWilkins.Me to get wholesale pricing.

More From Aly:

40 Day Sacred Wealth Ritual
A guided 40-day abundance ritual to attract more abundance into your life, utilizing the loving forces of Divinity while simultaneously re-programming your conditioning around abundance. This is a highly rated product and Aly's signature program. Learn more and get access at www.AlyWilkins.Me.

Akashic Record Readings
Visit www.AlyWilkins.Me to book your Akashic Record session with Aly. See the website for reviews and more information.

1:1 Spiritual Mentorship
E-mail AlyWilkinsAbundance@gmail.com to book your mentorship session with Aly. See www.AlyWilkins.Me for reviews and current offerings.

Group Retreats + Individual Retreats
See www.AlyWilkins.Me for up-to-date retreat offerings or e-mail AlyWilkinsAbundance@gmail.com if you'd like to book a private or group retreat.

DoTerra Oils
You can purchase DoTerra oils from Aly at www.AlyWilkins.Me to get wholesale pricing.

THANK YOU.

A special thank you to all of the Light Leaders who have come before me. Thank you for guiding the way and paving the path. I deeply honor and appreciate your commitment to the new paradigm of Love.

A special thank you to the Reader, for your commitment to becoming your Highest Self and honoring the Divinity within.

Always remember who you are.

TABLE OF CONTENTS

INTRODUCTION

Most of us grew up hearing that we should strive to make a lot of money, in hopes that money and success would make us happy. Yet we were riddled with beliefs and ways of being with money that did not support us in creating, attracting or holding onto our wealth. Having money means that you have options, which removes a lot of stress from your life and can create a lot of happiness! But money cannot bring you anything more than temporary happiness. What's underneath will always rise to the surface.

This is a book about creating abundance in your life, because that's the real form of wealth. The paradox is, that wealth really has nothing to do with abundance. Many are wealthy, but are not abundant. Money doesn't bring you a vibration of abundance - it's the opposite. We create the abundance first, and then the money flows in, because it has no choice but to do so when you are emitting a certain vibration out into the world. Abundance attracts material wealth as well as spiritual, emotional and mental wealth. When you hold a vibration of abundance, you can attract money to you in an instant, simply through your way of being.

The goal we're all after is to feel abundant in our day to day lives - we may think that we need money, money, money - but that just creates a game of constantly chasing something outside of you that can never create true happiness within. Chasing money stops you from being able to appreciate the massive wealth that is right in front of you.

In this book, you're going to learn how to activate the abundance that's already inside you! We'll address the physical, emotional and energetic blockages that may be slowing down the flow of abundance (and money) in your life so that you can begin feeling the full flow of abundance on a daily basis.

What we are doing in this book together is intense. Trust your intuition and however it leads you to read this. This is almost everything I've learned about abundance - and we're approaching it all at once. It took me years to fully work through all of the processes I share in this book, so don't expect yourself to be healed overnight. Come back to the sections that feel most resonant and take your time with it.

This is going to be a journey through your Soul - I personally recommend reading this multiple times so that the information can really soak into your cells and you can begin to embody this vibration working on the areas that you feel most drawn to healing at that time. When you're embodying the vibration, you'll notice that you just seem to attract things to you at the most aligned timing, consistently. You'll be able to release the mentality that money and wealth only comes to you through hard work and can be much easier and fulfilling.

Initially, I wanted to just write a book about spiritual wealth. Spirit led me to shift this into working through abundance energetically, working with the Chakra System. I specifically chose to publish this as a workbook, instead of a regular book, because actually going through the questions here is the whole point. If you skip the exercises, you don't need to read this book. This is a book about embodiment - not collecting more information. Don't we have enough of that already? In each section, I'll give you a quick lesson, but the healing only happens when you dive into how each lesson shows up for you in your life. That's where change and healing take place. Do each exercise - don't skip anything.

Commit this to yourself now.

I, _____, promise to show up fully for myself throughout this workbook. I will not skip sections because I think "I already know" or because the content makes me feel uncomfortable, too intense, or even confronted. I am willing to look at myself so that I can learn where I can create more room for abundance in my life.

I ask that you enter this container with a completely open mind. This is not your typical "make more money" book - it is actually probably unlike any book you've ever read. Take in everything with an open mind and leave what doesn't resonate with you. This is my truth, it may not necessarily be yours. However, I am right. Just kidding. I also hope to make you laugh throughout this book, because what is life without laughter? :)

Last note before we dive in: you'll find several free resources in the book that are available for you on my website - just visit www.AlyWilkins.Me to download them!

MY PERSONAL JOURNEY WITH ABUNDANCE + WEALTH

Before we officially get started, you may want to know a little bit about my story to understand more about where all of this came from.

Like most of us, I grew up with the society-implanted goal of doing well in school, so I could get into college, so I could get a good job, build a white picket fence and survive until I was 75 and retire. Then, it would be ok to do all the fun things I wanted to do and daydreamed about, but couldn't earlier in life because I was too busy studying or working or didn't have enough vacation days.

I spent hundreds of afternoon breaks in the bathroom at work, wondering "how is this my life," or having mental conversations that I wish I could have with my boss... "don't you feel like this is just a waste of your time, too? Don't you want to feel fulfilled? Does this really make your Soul happy?" I considered just running out to my car and never coming back dozens of times.

At 24 years old, I found myself extremely miserable and depressed, despite everything in my life looking like it was perfect and going along perfectly with "my plan". I had a "great" job at one of the largest companies in the world and lived in a beautiful apartment with a nice, shiny car sitting in the parking garage. The problem was, nothing about my life impressed me. I wasn't proud of myself. I honestly didn't even try very hard, or stretch myself in any way to create any of those things. I had followed society's plan for me instead of finding myself and figuring out what would make me happy and fulfilled.

I hit my breaking point and escaped away to Bali for two months, where I re-discovered so many parts of myself. From there, I embarked on a spiritual journey that continues to unravel in which I allow my heart and soul to guide my life. We all have incredibly unique callings and things that make us happy - and it's so important to listen to those and lead life from the heart.

During this whole process, I started to learn how to attract more money to support my soul desires and create the fulfillment I had been yearning for. I worked my way up the corporate ladder so that I could invest more in learning about who I was here to be, what I really wanted to do with my life and how I would feel most fulfilled. What I learned was that money is only filling a void that we have inside - it is abundance that we are truly seeking.

I went on a rampage for about two years of reading about everything I could get my hands on when it came to finances, investing, being a responsible human financially - you name it, I read it. What I found was that 90% of the material I read had the same boring, cookie-cutter advice and it felt like something huge was missing. If it was just as easy as saving, budgeting and investing - wouldn't we all be rich by now? That's when I became obsessed with learning about the psychological and spiritual side of money - attracting money to us through our way of being and our vibration. Diving into the ancient wisdom of working with the energy of money deeply inspired me and shifted my life.

   Through years of studies and embodying this work, I feel ready to release *Sacred Wealth*. As our world is shifting so quickly, it feels imperative to begin living life from a space of abundance, not lack. To live life from our heart, not from the mind. From the 5D, not the 3D. This book will help support you in doing so - and help you to radiate the vibration of abundance so you can attract what you desire with much more ease.

CREATING THE CONTAINER FOR MAGIC

It's time to set our intention for this container. Bringing intention to everything we do is one of the big principles we'll be discussing throughout this book. Awareness and intention are literally everything. Without it, we're just floating through life, manifesting aimlessly and unknowingly creating our world from our subconscious minds.

What was your initial intention when you saw and purchased this book? What made you want to pick it up?

What would you like to shift in your life financially?

What do you hope to learn or embody deeper by reading this book?

The Chakra System

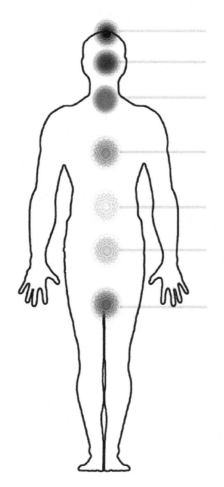

Crown Chakra
Third Eye Chakra
Throat Chakra

Heart Chakra

Solar Plexus Chakra

Sacral Chakra

Root Chakra

THE CHAKRA SYSTEM

The Chakra System is a powerful energetic system that runs throughout our body as well as outside of it. Chakras are known as "wheels of energy" that keep us in balance and energetically flowing. We'll be focusing on the 7 main chakras within our bodies in this book.

Imagine a spinning wheel inside your body and when it is in alignment, this wheel keeps your energy flowing beautifully and harmonically. However, when it's out of alignment, it slows down and blocks certain energy from moving through, making you feel like something is off. This is similar to a hose - when it's flowing freely, water comes out with ease. If you're stepping on the hose or folding it, you're restricting a lot of that flow that wants to come to you, but is stuck.

When we feel out of balance, it's likely because our chakras are out of alignment. Learning about these chakras will help inform so much about your body and your energy and help bring you back to balance.

For example:
- If you constantly have digestive problems, you likely have an imbalance in your Root or Sacral Chakra.
- If all of your illnesses center around your throat, your Throat Chakra is probably out of whack.
- If you can't get vulnerable or let anyone in, your Heart Chakra could have gigantic gates around it that block love from coming in and being received.
- When you feel powerless or like you aren't worthy, your Solar Plexus is calling for some loving and rebalancing.

There are **7 main chakras** within the body that we'll be diving into, one by one :

- Root Chakra (Muladhara)
- Sacral Chakra (Swadhisthana)
- Solar Plexus Chakra (Manipura)
- Heart Chakra (Anahata)
- Throat Chakra (Vishuddha)
- Third Eye Chakra (Ajna)
- Crown Chakra (Sahasrara)

We'll begin with the Root Chakra.

Root Chakra

Mūlādhāra

Root Chakra

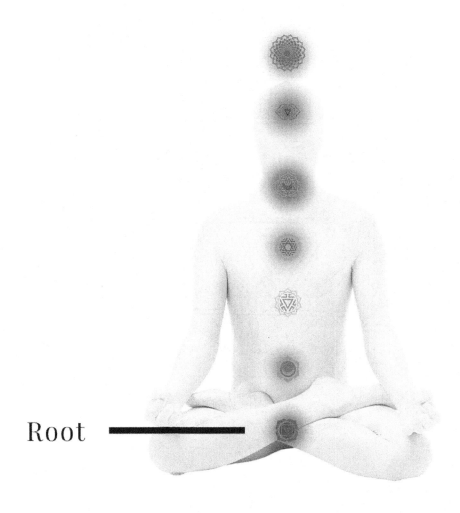

Root ————

ROOT CHAKRA: MULADHARA

Everything begins with the Root. Our root is our stability, our safety, our groundedness - it supports us feeling secure in the world and in our bodies. The Root Chakra is located at the base of the Spine and is representative of survival.

In regards to the conversation of Abundance and Sacred Wealth - the Root Chakra is where we hold many ancient beliefs, programs, patterns, fears and more from our ancestral line as well as from our own life.

Have you heard of generational womb trauma? When we are bathing in our mother's wombs, we are literally soaking up her cellular beliefs - so oftentimes, we carry beliefs that are not even ours, maybe not even our mothers but beliefs of our ancestors.

These beliefs won't magically disappear until we shine a light on them and create awareness around if that belief serves us anymore.

Do you want the belief system of your great-grandmother who raised her children during the Great Depression or times of great famine? It's not that we disown these beliefs, it's that we look at them and determine if they are helpful today or not. Many beliefs carry much wisdom but may not be appropriate in modern times or require great discernment.

This chapter's work is all about creating a feeling of safety in your finances as well as creating supportive beliefs that will allow you to far surpass your dreams. This could be very intense - trust that the healing process is working and allow any emotions that want to rise to the surface to emerge. When we push our emotions away, we're just pushing them into a crevice in our body to store and then it can result in dis-ease and much more. Remember, feeling your emotions is safe and healthy to do. We have to feel them to move through them.

If you face anything that you need support or a virtual hug with, I am just an e-mail away at alywilkinsabundance@gmail.com or check the book resources at www.AlyWilkins.Me.

Whatever I believe about money will manifest.

#SacredWealth

ABUNDANCE PRINCIPLE 1: IDENTIFY YOUR ROOT BELIEFS

When we are born, we come as (mostly) blank slates. We don't come into the world with any beliefs - we are taught the beliefs that those around us think to be true. As we grow older, the people who are around us hopefully provide a safe home and a nurturing space for us to learn and experience life. While those caregivers usually have the best of intentions, it doesn't mean that what they are teaching us is true. It's only "true" in their experience.

From the ages of 0-7, we are literally sponges. We absorb the energy our caregivers emit and trust what they say is true, without having any real means of discernment yet. That means that we absorb many wonderful beliefs, as well as harmful ones. What your parents or caregivers taught you is probably what they were taught as children. The scary part is, it's easy to go throughout life without ever evaluating your beliefs, since for the most part, they are subconscious. Can you imagine getting your guidance around money from someone who was born during the Great Depression? Times have changed so much since then!

Think about how you grew up - what was the vibe in your house around money? How did your caregivers talk about money in general? What would you have picked up on as a child?

I always use this example when working with clients - consider how the Kardashian children will think of money and what they will learn about money management. Compare that to a middle class child, who grows up watching their parents work incredibly hard to put food on the table. Compare that to someone who grows up in an orphanage and has no real context of money, except what they see and hear from their peers and authority figures. Compare that to someone who grows up seeing their parent work 4 jobs to keep food on the table.

> **Nothing about money is ultimately true - other than that is ENERGY.**

Two people could both feel 100% right in their justification around money.

As individuals, it's our job to become aware of what kind of environments we grew up in around money and how that has impacted our relationship with money and our financial life. It's the first step of attaining true wealth.

If we skip this, you could earn millions of dollars next week, but you will have programming and conditioning running your ways of being with money that may affect those earnings. You see constantly on the news " lottery winner goes bankrupt!" It's not about the money. It's about our way of being with money.

So, let's get to dissecting. I want you to look at this as a harmless, painless audit looking into your ways of being with money. There is no judgment. Pretend you were looking over this with a friend - and have the same level of compassion you would have for someone you adore and love dearly when you do these practices with yourself.

Wanting to create a more powerful and intentional relationship with money is important work - and it can be confronting. I'm proud of you for stepping in and being willing to be vulnerable so that you can grow and experience even more abundance and freedom.

We will start with a simple list of fill-in-the-blanks to see what you truly believe about money. This exercise is a great way to get a baseline view of where your frequency is at right now in relation to money. Answer the following questions with the first word that pops in your head. It's important you are very honest here - no one will see this but you. This is how we get an accurate gauge of what our relationship to money looks like (so we have to be REAL!) There are no right or wrong answers here.

Money is _____.

Rich people are _____.

My mother taught me that money is _____.

When I have money, I feel _____.

The most important lesson I've learned about money is _____.

What I really desire with money is _____.

When I see someone living my dream life, I feel _____.

I use money as an excuse as to why I'm not _____.

My biggest dream I haven't moved forward on because of money is _____.

When I check my bank account, I feel _____.

My father is _____ with his money.

You have to _____ to make money.

Money only shows up for _____ people.

It takes _____ to have money.

Money _____ me.

My experience of money is _____.

Money, at its core, is _____.

Wealthy people are _____ with money.

Poor people are _____ with money.

People who make millions of dollars a year are _____.

What do you notice in these responses? Does anything surprise you?

What is your first memory of money?

What has your experience of money been like, in general?

How did money impact your life when you were growing up?

What did you know about or hear about money growing up?

What did your mother teach you about money?

What did your father teach you about money?

What was your family's experience of money growing up?

How did the people who raise you talk about others regarding money? (think teachers, fire fighters, athletes, musicians, CEO's, etc).

Take a quick look over your answers in the last few pages. What's the overall vibe in your answers?

Now, take a deep breath. Let it go.

Our beliefs inform the Universe of what to deliver to our reality.

#SacredWealth

ABUNDANCE PRINCIPLE 2 : AUDIT YOUR BELIEF SYSTEM

We all have tens of thousands of beliefs that guide our way through life and help to keep us "safe". Most of these beliefs are subconscious and we don't consciously know we're going through life with them. Some are more obvious to us.

Whatever we believe, we all know we want to be right. So when innately we want to be accurate, our subconscious minds will literally search the field for evidence of what we believe to be true and attract that to us. What we focus on, we find and we attract!

Today's work is about conducting an audit of our beliefs around money and abundance. As we grow, we always want to monitor the beliefs flowing through us to make sure they are serving the type of life we want to create!

Our beliefs inform our thoughts and feelings, which direct our actions.

So if you believe that "women are bad at managing money" - you are basically only going to see examples of women losing money, mismanaging their finances, losing everything, causing massive financial havoc, and other "proof" to solidify your beliefs. If you're a woman, you'll likely see this within yourself. If you are not female, you'll attract females in your life with these stories as partners, friends, lovers, etc.

If you believe that you have to be incredibly smart to make money, and you don't think you are incredibly smart, you will likely self-sabotage any opportunity that comes to you to create money because you aren't a match for those opportunities with that belief. You'll attract opportunities that confirm your false belief that you are not smart.

If you believe that you have to work hard to create money, you aren't going to make any money unless you work your ass off, constantly. When you take a break, you won't make money.

Can you see how important it is that we know what beliefs are running our worlds?

Our beliefs inform the Universe of what to deliver in our lives.

They are the most important place to start when we want to grow in any area of our life.

Whenever I want to decipher if a belief is harmful or helpful, I'll ask myself the following questions:

- How does this belief make me feel?

- Does this feel empowering or disempowering?

- Would I want this belief to be the direction for my life?

In our previous exercise, you wrote down a few things you believe about money. Take a look back at those responses and write down your top 3 harmful beliefs about money as well as your top beneficial beliefs about money.

Top Harmful Beliefs About Money:

1.

2.

3.

Now we want to shift those harmful beliefs into more empowering beliefs. Let's say we are working through a belief that " I can only make money when I work really hard at something."

Step 1: Ask if it is True in all situations and circumstances.

No, that's absolutely not true. Billionaires of the world make more money every day than they could ever spend, without doing literally anything. The systems they set up and their employees are working for them. The guy who invented Pool Noodles is probably just sitting back enjoying life. Jennifer Aniston makes tons of money every year from reruns of Friends! This is not true in all situations.

> **Step 2 :** Completely discredit the belief. Step out of the belief and declare it - rediculous. When we make something funny, it has a fast way of losing power within us.

It's kind of funny that I forgot about people who make money with such ease. There are dog walkers in New York City who make $200,000 a year, walking dogs 5 times a week (a previous client of mine brought this to my attention years ago. It's true)! There are restaurant owners bringing in massive revenue from the employees who manage their franchises and they haven't worked in 10 years. There are entrepreneurs and consultants who work 10 hours a week and make more money than they did in their strenuous 9 to 5 jobs. There are influencers making money from sharing toothpaste. It's confirmed - this is a ridiculous belief.

> **Step 3:** What has this story cost you so far?

All beliefs create positive and negative effects on your life. Believing that the only way to make money is working hard costs you so much: hours of your time daily, your mental health and even physical aspects of your health such as adrenal fatigue. Burnout and overworking often lead to significant health issues. This story is costing you a significant amount.

> **Step 4:** Shift into a different belief that feels true for you.

We want to create a belief that feels true inside. Your subconscious will automatically reject anything that feels false. You want to ease yourself into something that feels true. So you might not say "I am a millionaire!" if you have $0.70 in your bank account, but your subconscious could get on board with examples like this:
- "The energy of money feels exciting to me."
- " I believe that money wants to support me."
- "I am open to believing that money can come to me with ease."

Do you feel how that gives you some room to grow into the new belief and still calls in the vibration you're wanting to feel with money?

Ok, your turn! Use the next few pages to shift the beliefs that aren't serving you anymore to something that can help you in expanding your mindset.

Shift Belief #1 from Disempowering to Empowering

Old Belief:

1. Is this belief ultimately true?

2. Discredit the belief and see why it's laughable.

3. What has this story cost you?

4. Create a new, more empowering belief that feels honest.

Shift Belief #2 from Disempowering to Empowering

Old Belief:

1. Is this belief ultimately true?

2. Discredit the belief and see why it's laughable.

3. What has this story cost you?

4. Create a new, more empowering belief that feels honest.

Shift Belief #3 from Disempowering to Empowering

Old Belief:

1. Is this belief ultimately true?

2. Discredit the belief and see why it's laughable.

3. What has this story cost you?

4. Create a new, more empowering belief that feels honest.

Great work dismantling some old, dusty ass beliefs that don't belong in your life anymore!

I recommend putting your new beliefs on post-it notes around your house, in your car, on the refrigerator or even creating an alarm on your phone with the new belief.

Our money story influences how we are with money, but as soon as we recognize that it's our responsibility to take our power back and do the work to create the shifts we want to see.

What is your experience with money right now?

What are your biggest challenges financially right now?

In general, how do you relate to money? What emotions come up most often for you when dealing with your finances (paying bills, getting paid, shopping, buying necessities, gifts, etc).

There are going to be different stories and beliefs about money, as a collective, as we travel across the world. I'm writing from the United States, so I'd like to cover some of the most common money blocks I see with clients and in society - and help you debunk them!

Some of these are so subconscious, you don't even realize that they're floating around in your psyche in some way.

***** THESE ARE NOT TRUE IN ANY WAY*****

- FALSE : When I make money, it means someone else is making less.
  - There is more than enough for everyone to go around. The system we operate in likes to fool us and act like there's not enough. There is more than enough.

- RIDICULOUS: You have to work hard and do whatever it takes to be successful financially.
  - What about the girl who makes $300K a year dog walking in New York City?
  - What about the guy who invented the snuggie??
  - How about the person who loves what they do and makes more money doing it than they did at their old job they hated?

- ABSOLUTE LIE: I don't deserve to make a lot of money.
  - You were born, so you are deserving of whatever you desire! All you have to do is hold the vision and act on the inspiration that comes in.

- PREPOSTEROUS: There's not enough to go around for everyone. We live in a limited world.
  - Nope, nope, nope. Plenty for everyone to go around.

- INACCURATE: I don't really want the responsibility of earning a lot of money.
  - It's also a heavy responsibility to not know how you'll make rent next month. Pretty sure you'll be happy taking calls from your dream home and delegating that work to your accountant or money manager. Which is easier?

- UNTRUE: Paying taxes is the worst and I don't want to give the government that much money.
  - You can hire a really great accountant who can help you minimize your tax payments and support causes that do matter to you with your financial abundance.

- OPTIONAL: If I make more money, I have to help everyone around me and I don't want to.
  - You can do whatever you want with your money. You can be as public or as private about it as you want to be. No rules here!

Please put this on Post It Notes all around your house....

> Money is just energy. Whatever beliefs I have about money will manifest.

What blocks or beliefs do you feel are most in your way of attracting the money and abundance you truly desire? It might feel like you can't shake this belief.
Example: No matter how much money I have, I always seem to carry debt.

What makes you believe that this block/belief is accurate?

Is that belief ultimately true?

Does that belief help you reach your goals or hurt your ability to meet your goal?

With the beliefs that feel deeply rooted, I like to counteract them with powerful "I AM" statements in addition to new beliefs that are more supportive.

A few examples of powerful "I Am" Statements:

- I am intuitive and trust my inner guidance.
- I am great at managing my money.
- I am happy to ask for help when I have a question.
- I am a quick learner.
- I am a money magnet.
- I am abundant and attract magic everywhere I go.
- I am resourceful and resilient.
- I am trusting that the right people will always show up on my path and I'll receive the guidance that's required in the moment.
- I am guided.

What is the current "I AM" statement that you're saying in your head regarding this belief? Ex: I am always leaking money when I overdraft my account and it doesn't feel good.

```



```

How can you shift this "I AM" Statement to create a powerful new reality for yourself?
Ex: I am resilient, capable and powerful beyond my imagination. I am resourceful.

```



```

Something you can do to make this statement feel more real for you, is add something like " I am open to believing that...." or "I am seeing possibilities that ...."

- I am learning to be a money magnet
- I am open to attracting massive amounts of money
- I am available for creative ideas to generate money

We are reprogramming our brain here, so we want to make sure our inputs are actually going through, especially if we spend a lot of time on them.

To check in, you can ask "do I really feel this inside my bones?"

Your subconscious patterns can easily sabatoge your experience of money.

#SacredWealth

ABUNDANCE PRINCIPLE 3: SHINE AWARENESS ON YOUR PATTERNS

Many of us have patterns with money. Like our beliefs, some of our patterns are beneficial and some are not. It's important that we can get honest and take a look at the patterns that are affecting our lives now, so that we can shift them if they are not serving us. Here are a few examples of common patterns I see most in regards to spending money:

- Shopping to make us feel happier or to distract us
- Swiping your credit card, but never looking at your statement (denial monster)
- Missing bills and payments often and paying a lot in late fees
- Buying the cheapest option so you can save as much money as possible
- Buying the most expensive option so you get the highest quality or get the status
- Judging others based on how they spend their money
- Feeling guilty about purchases you've made or want to make

None of these are wrong or right - we just have to look at them clearly so we can see when they are helpful and when they are not. Once we recognize that a pattern may not be the best for us, we can transform it!

Let's look at a few examples of when a pattern could be beneficial sometimes and problematic in other situations:

- Buying something nice for yourself or treating yourself to something special when you've had a rough week. This is a kind act of self-love, occasionally, but if it's done every time you have a slightly bad day, it could create more damage as it's created a coping mechanism for you to avoid your feelings. There could be another habit that would help you cope in a less costly way!

- The person who always looks for the cheapest option. If you're at a store with many overpriced brands, but the product quality is the same, than this habit will save you a lot of money! However, occasionally you could actually save more money in the long run by purchasing certain items at a higher price that would mean it is higher quality. For example: when I buy leggings from TJ Maxx, they usually get a hole in them (or I notice they are see through, ugh) after a year of wear, but if I buy LuluLemon leggings, they last me 5 years for 3x the price. Ultimately, the Lulu's are a better purchase for my long legs if I have the additional cash for them.

Continual patterns are the ones that can cause the most damage, when we aren't using them wisely. A few years ago, I realized that I had a habit of buying too many books on Amazon. I'd always end up having a stack 20 books high on my nightstand and felt overwhelmed even looking at them.

When I thought about how much money I was spending and the books weren't even getting read, I realized something needed to shift. Learning and growth is one of my biggest values, so I didn't want to completely stop buying books, but I set up a few rules that would support me instead of hurt me:

- Books must stay in the cart for 7 days and then I will decide if I want to order it or not (how often do you change your mind with small purchases?!)
- I only order books when I have less than 2 books on my bookshelf that I have not read.

These "rules" helped me to save money and spend much more intentionally. It also eliminated the overwhelm I felt when looking at that giant stack of books on my nightstand. Win/Win!

Here are a couple of other examples of shifts I've made to my ineffective patterns with spending that have really supported me - I call them my Abundance Rules :

- <u>Waiting Time to buy anything!</u> Usually it's a week or a month, depending on how big it is. Great advice I heard from a mentor was to wait a YEAR to buy any huge purchase once you start creating more money. That way, in a year, you may not even want that high ticket item anymore and if you do, it will be that much more special.

- <u>I have a list of ready to go questions that I ask whenever I purchase anything</u>. These help me determine if I really want something, or if my ego just wants instant gratification:
  - Do I already have this?
  - Do I have something like this or that looks like this already?
  - Do I actually need this? Will I want it in 2 years, or will it be in a junk drawer?
  - Does this bring me joy?

- <u>Practicing appreciation when I purchase anything!</u> "Thank you to the driver who transported this beautiful dress to this store, thank you to the Uber driver who dropped me off here, thank you to the person who designed this dress in such beautiful colors", etc.

Let's take a look at the specific patterns that are affecting your life right now. The point of this exercise is not to judge yourself or feel bad, it's to get aware of the patterns that you know about right now and could use a little tidying up.

What patterns can see within yourself that may be harmful, when you really get honest?

Where do these patterns come from? (It's not always necessary to know where, but if we can spot it is is helpful in identifying the root of the issue).

How could you shift this pattern so that it serves you more?

What are a few Abundance Rules you could create to support you in overcoming this pattern?

I had a really wonderful boss when I worked in a city called Altamonte Springs. One day, the owners took our team out for lunch at a nearby mall followed by dessert. Then he said, "SURPRISE! Each of you are getting a gift card to the mall. You have the next two hours to shop and get something special for yourself."

What's so interesting is how differently everyone spent those gift cards:

- One spent the full gift card at the first store she went to, then saw something else she wanted, but had spent her giftcard so used her debit card.
- Another looked at every store she was interested in, and then went back to the stores where she really wanted something and purchased it.
- Someone else saved their gift card to give to someone else for a gift!
- Another person sold their gift card online so they could get cash, since they really didn't want anything at the mall anyways.

None of these examples are the "right" option - every scenario has a different answer that would be most effective. You might think that "giving a gift card to a friend as a gift" is the "right" answer there - but the gift was actually for them and they didn't fully receive it. Giving is always wonderful, but not when we are doing it to deflect receiving on our own. Women do this all the time. We get to take care of ourselves first, allow ourselves to receive, and give from the overflow. Or, maybe she was receiving as she got to then keep her cash that she would've used for the gift! None of this is black and white - it's all nuanced.

How do you think you would spend this gift card in this scenario? Do one of these patterns fit your behaviors when shopping?

Most of us have some patterns when it comes to spending - some helpful and some harmful! In the example above, I was the person who went to every store and then evaluated what I wanted. Great for my wallet, annoying for my friends, and takes more time. Harmful in some ways, helpful in others. We get to discern when something works and when it doesn't. That's a helpful habit when I'm making a big purchase, but a total waste of time when I'm trying to decide which brand of paper clips to get.

An old habit that I squashed years ago was buying cheap clothes online when I was bored or felt like I didn't have enough (my bulging closet would have stated otherwise).

I conducted an experiment to see what would happen - I started shopping online, but skipping the checkout process. I'd have fun looking at all the clothes, adding to my cart, etc - and then stop. I'd leave the clothes in the cart for a week or so, and if I still wanted them, I would purchase them then! Eventually, I drastically reduced the amount of money I spent on clothes because it just wasn't important to me! I would look at the clothes online and enjoy the shopping process, but realize that was all the fun I wanted, and if something really stuck in my mind then I would buy it later.

Later, I realized that saving those 6 shopping sprees in a year allowed me to instead buy a round-trip plane ticket to Bali. That was much more fun for me than some new clothes, since traveling is one of my highest excitements.

The more you appreciate the money flowing in, the more will want to come.

#SacredWealth

ABUNDANCE PRINCIPLE 4: GET CLEAR ON WHERE YOU'RE AT

Today is one of the most important principles - and one of the most practical when it comes to handling your physical wealth. If you're committed to financial abundance, this is a step that you cannot skip, no matter how much it might make you nervous or want to run away.

The energy of money is very feminine and flowing throughout the ethers, but we live on Planet Earth, so while we must learn how to energetically work with money, we also get to learn how to care for it in a grounded manner.

The first step is taking your head out of the sand. Some of us know exactly what's in our bank accounts and wallets, to the penny, and others might put their bills in the freezer, like Andy in Parks + Rec. Wherever you're at is perfectly ok - and I want you to acknowledge yourself for doing this work now. Be proud of yourself.

In order to manage our physical wealth efficiently, we need to know what we're working with. The wealthiest people in the world always know what is in their bank account.

We're going to get really clear about what you have in your accounts currently, what you owe and where you may not want to be looking.

How much money do you have in assets (anything you own or could sell to earn money - bank accounts, savings accounts, retirement, cars, property, etc)? List these out by line item.

```



```

What do you owe in liabilities (anything you are borrowing or paying off - student loans, debt, car loans, mortgages, etc)?

```



```

Do you have savings accounts? What are they for? Are they earning interest?

Are you investing in a retirement account regularly? Do you have one? What's the max you can be allocating each year? Does your employer match your contributions or any part of them?

I created a running spreadsheet that you can use for this - you can find it on my website www.AlyWilkins.Me in the Book Resources section. You can make a copy of the spreadsheet and reuse it every time you check in on your finances, so it's easy to track how things have been shifting.

After you've gotten clear about what's happening in your current financial life, I want you to give yourself a big hug!! Many people don't take the time to do this and choose to live in denial, instead. Getting clear on where you're at is the first step to attracting what you want!

Create Supportive Systems + Rituals to Stay Clear!

Another way that we honor money is by consistently paying attention to it. Getting clear just once isn't enough - we want to have a daily, weekly or monthly practice to get clear with where we are at and cultivate excitement about where we are going! It's important to know what is in your accounts at all times! Wealthy people always know what's in their accounts. Denial is not your friend when it comes to finances.

I recommend that you choose one day of the week to start checking in with your money regularly. I love "Wealthy Wednesdays" or "Freedom Fridays!" In this time, you want to cultivate a short routine that helps you get in touch with where you're at and where you are going. Go into each account, look at the balance and say "thank you, thank you, thank you!!" It doesn't matter what is in there - we are blessed to have abundance in whatever form it looks like. Even if you are in the negative - you have a bank account that allows you to grow a lot of money! Practicing gratitude here is vital.

I personally recommend using your same spreadsheet from the "Getting Clear" Exercise and just add a column for the date so that you can track this in one place every week and access it anywhere you are. What I would suggest is having one section for your Assets (anything you own), another section for your Liabilities (anything you owe) and a final section for Savings + Investments. Each week, I write the amount present in each account, which helps me stay on track with what's happening in my finances.

Another fun thing to do is add a column for Manifested Money. Keep track of any money you manifested in the last week - think free gift cards, coupons, a friend bought your coffee, etc.

You want this to feel fun, sacred, activating and empowering! I love to make some hot tea, light a candle, burn some incense and play my favorite music. Maybe you put on your salt lamp and pour a glass of champagne. Whatever makes you feel high vibe and abundant. The most important part about this weekly ritual is that you are in a high vibration. Sometimes it can be easy to feel discouraged when we look at our finances if we haven't met the goals we have for ourselves - but the trick is to always approach this exercise with appreciation and high vibrations. If we look at our money from a low vibration, we're going to keep attracting more of it. We'll talk a lot more about this effect later in the book. Stay tuned!

How often will you now check in with your Finances? Put it in your calendar so this will actually happen!

How will you make that process special and Sacred?

Check-in with your body right now. What's happening? Is there any resistance or fear to this? Is there boredom? What's coming up for you?

Reminder: the more you appreciate the money flowing in, the more will want to come.

When money feels
like it will be well
utilized, with loving
energy and intention,
it will flow in.

#SacredWealth

ABUNDANCE PRINCIPLE 5: CREATE A FEELING OF SAFETY

We'll be talking a lot in this book about seeing our connection with money as a relationship. For any relationship to last, both parties have to feel safe! Today, we are going to be exploring how you can feel more safe earning and saving money as well as how you can manage your money in a way that fully utilizes its power!

Everyone wants to feel safe with their significant other. Once that trust has been broken, it becomes more difficult to build back and takes some solid effort, right? If Sally's husband hurts her, it's going to take more than one "i'm sorry" to fix it. He is going to have to show changed behavior to help Sally feel safe again. She wants to trust him!! She just has to see that he has actually shifted and she won't get hurt or disappointed again. Money feels the same way. When it feels like it will be well utilized, with loving energy and intention, it will flow in with ease!

When you know you'll be taken care of, you feel much safer with someone and are more trusting, right? That's the dynamic we're creating with our Abundance.

Time to tune in - ***in what ways are you actually afraid of creating more money?*** You may read that and laugh - who would be AFRAID of making money?! You'd be surprised!

Often we have deep subconscious fears about what happens when we become wealthier:

- Way too much responsibility! I can't handle that pressure!
- More money, more problems mentality
- I don't even want to think about paying taxes when I'm making X Figures
- Will my friends still like me if I start making more money than them?
- What will my family say about me making more money?
- Will I have to give money to everyone if I'm making more than them?
- What if people take advantage of me when I get wealthy?
- Will I change and become a total snob if I'm rich?
- How will I shift when I make more money? What if I become greedy?

These subconscious thoughts can live under the surface and affect our ability to receive until we actually become aware of them. For example, one fear I used to have was that I would start to become greedy if I created more money. I told some of my clients that at a previous retreat, hoping they wouldn't judge me. They all busted out laughing, like "Aly, what are you talking about?! You are so generous - that is ridiculous to even think." That belief IS absolutely crazy and I have know idea where it came from.

Sometimes beliefs don't even stem from our own lifetimes - when we don't resonate with a belief or understand why it's in us, it could have been absorbed through ancestral wounding, womb trauma or even a past life. We don't need to know the origin, but we do need to get clear about what we're scared of so we can fully let it go!

When you think about yourself making your DREAM amount of money -- does anything scare you about that? (Be real. Something does, or you would be earning that income right now.)

That fear that comes up when you think about living in your full abundance - does this support you, or push you away from abundance? Is that belief even true? Is it a "likely" or "realistic" belief? Is it laughable? Prove it wrong.

What would make you feel "safe" financially?

How could you create that?

What's stopping you from creating it right now?

One of my favorite self-help finance books, *The Richest Man of Babylon*, as well as many other books speak on the value of paying yourself first. The author says "What did YOU keep from what you earned last month?" I'm not sure about you, but I never learned that in school. I learned that I pay my bills so my credit score doesn't suffer, and I will keep whatever is left over. The problem with that scenario is that you pay everyone else without ever giving yourself anything and it can lead to the "paycheck to paycheck" lifestyle very quickly.

I recommend you start paying yourself first, even if it's just 5% of your paycheck. Ideally you can autodraft 10-20% of your income each month into a separate account that's just for you, but start with whatever you can. Put it into a *contingency fund*. We don't call it an Emergency Fund, because that will literally attract emergencies to you. Our brain is confused by the word "Contingency" and it serves the same purpose, but won't manifest disaster! I personally write out my bills all on one sheet of paper for reference and pay my "Contingency Bill" every month when I pay my rent.

Eventually, you can allocate more money to this and divide it between retirement accounts, savings accounts and other funds that are important to you. I literally have a savings account for Beyonce concerts... you can create savings funds for anything!! I personally love Capital

One 360's savings accounts for short-term savings because you can create several funds under one umbrella account and are able to label each one : Christmas Fund, Birthday Gifts fund, Beyonce Fund, Laptop Fund, Travel Fund, etc. This is similar to the old envelope trick, but your money will earn a little bit of interest (and you won't lose the envelope!)

Do you pay yourself first, or pay your bills first? Why?

```



```

How much can you allocate to putting into a Contingency Account every week, bi-weekly or monthly?

```



```

Ok, harsh truth time. Do you spend more than you earn? In today's world, it's so easy, with ads literally targeting people by age, income, interests, credit card purchase history, movies they watch, places they visit, and a million more criteria. I used to create these ads for one of the biggest companies in the world and it is literally scary how refined you can get in your targeting, to find someone who will most likely purchase your product.

> *"Wealth, like a tree, grows from a tiny seed.*
> *You will be tempted, but I wisely refrained.*
> *Learn to live upon less than you earn."*
> - George Clason; Richest Man of Babylon

Do you find that you regularly spend more than you earn?

```



```

What areas are these in?

How could you shift this behavior?

What Abundance Rules could you create that would support you?

Take care of your money
like you would a child.
Don't let it run off without
knowing where it is going.

#SacredWealth

ABUNDANCE PRINCIPLE 6: FIND THE PHYSICAL MONEY LEAKS

Imagine a faucet running. Underneath the sink, there's a leak in the pipe and half of the water is rushing out with force. Think about all that water that's wasted! The same can happen with our financial health, so let's take today to address anything that should not be coming out of your account.

First of all, let's take Senior Investigator Rude F. Dickbag off of this project and approach this with compassion instead. We ALL have areas that money is leaking away from us, until we become aware and patch up those holes so we can be more efficient and thoughtful in how we share our financial abundance!

The most common money leakages:
- Subscriptions that are automatically paid each month that you completely forgot about
- Spending more than you think you are in certain areas (food, food and food)
- Losing money from investment fees, late fees or banking fees
- Giving or helping someone/something else at the expense of yourself
- Having the audacity to go to Target
- Buying many low-cost purchases that add up (more than you think they do)

Which are the areas that you're leaking money right now?
Remember, none of this is bad! You are getting aware so you can create something amazing out of this experience of learning how to play with money most effectively (and magically).

The only way we can really get clear on how we are spending is to look at the data.

So much of this is just becoming aware about what feels fun and exciting to spend money on - and what feels like an obligation, too much, or regret!

Step 1: Open up your bank accounts and print out all of your statements from the last 3 months.

Step 2: Highlight any expenses that are not survival-based. (PS fun purchases are wonderful but we just want to first get clear on what is survival and what is not). Survival = food, shelter, water.

Step 3: Look at your highlights. Does anything surprise you? Were you still paying for anything you didn't know about?

Which areas are you spending the most money on in the last 3 months?

Do these categories feel like aligned spending, based on your values?

If you could, would you have changed any of these purchase decisions? Why? What would you have done differently?

[ ]

Do you think you actually should be spending more money in any areas? (ex: when I did this the first time, I realized I had a very low expenditure on Health related items and that I would actually like to spend more on making sure I'm as healthy as possible).

[ ]

   The next part of this is equally as important. For the remainder of our work together (or atleast for 30 days, I want you to track everything you spend. This is going to be so enlightening!!

Get a notebook and write down the following anytime you spend money:

Date	Company	Purchase	Method of Payment	Cost
4/28/2020	VW	Car Payment	Debit	$222
5/1/2020	Rent	LA Rent	Debit	$1900
5/1/2020	Amazon	298 Books	Credit	$700
5/5/2020	Whole Foods	1 half-filled bag	Debit	$200

   At the end of each week, take a look at your spending tracker and see how much you're spending! Many of us are most shocked at what we spend on food, transportation and impulse purchases!

   I do this about once a year now, and the first time I did this exercise, I saw a massive spending pattern at Target and Amazon, so I said "no Target for 6 months" and realized how much I was impulse buying while I was there! Then, I gave myself my personal Amazon Book Rule - I only purchase books if I have less than 2 on my nightstand I haven't read, and I only purchase books if they have been in my cart at least a week and I still want them.

Before you begin tracking, where do you think you spend the most money?

Now, let's get to tracking! I suggest simply designating a notebook for your expenses, and write any expense down as soon as you spend it. Keeping this notebook in your purse or even a piece of paper in your wallet will make this extra convenient. You can also track this on your phone or online - whatever works for you.

After you track for 30 days, what did you notice?

Where are you spending more money or less money than you thought?

What changes feel appropriate to make after tracking your spending for 30 days?

What money do you spend that doesn't reflect your goals? (For example, are you saying you want to travel the world, but you're spending all your money at Anthropologie?)

What companies are you supporting the most with your purchases?

What Abundance Rules could you create for yourself that will support you?

For example, I have a "1 week rule" for non-essential items and if I want something, it says in the cart for at least a week. Often, I change my mind and decide I don't even want it anymore. This rule wasn't created to save money - but to reduce the junk in my house! I no longer have anything I don't absolutely love - everything I have is intentional. It needs to bring me joy. Nothing mediocre comes home with me.

Everything is always happening for your highest alignment.

#SacredWealth

ABUNDANCE PRINCIPLE 7: CHOOSE POWERFUL PERSPECTIVES

We can choose to view life through a victim perspective or through a loving perspective.

The victim perspective looks like:
- Life is happening TO me
- Poor me, life has been so hard on me
- Why does this always happen to me?
- Feel sorry for me - listen to this story about someone else who hurt me
- Someone else is to blame for how I feel
- It isn't my fault, it's their fault

There is no experience of abundance when we're operating from a victim mindset.

A powerful perspective looks like:
- Life is happening FOR me
- What can I learn from this?
- How can I grow from this?
- Why is this showing up for me?
- What's here for me?
- I'm thankful to learn this lesson.

When we have a core belief that everything is always happening for our highest alignment, it allows us to grow at a very fast pace. We start to see everything as a blessing. We start to see the challenges of life as a necessary stepping stone to the future we're asking for (and they are). Abundance pours into our lives when we view life from this perspective. After all, everything is happening FOR us!

> The loving perspective supports you feeling good.
> The loving perspective supports your growth.
> The loving perspective supports your happiness.

To shift from the victim mindset to the powerful, loving perspective requires us to take complete responsibility and ownership of our lives. There is no more blaming allowed. You attract everything to you - or it is happening for a reason.

A few examples of shifting our paradigm:

- Relationship ending.
  - <u>Victim:</u> What a waste of my time! Why didn't we realize it wasn't our highest alignment earlier? Now I have to start all over.

- - Powerful: What an experience! I'm so grateful to have learned so many lessons. I'm really thankful that I got to experience this so I could receive clarity on what I desire in the future. This will support me as I start dating again.

- "I hate my job. I am overworked."
  - Victim: My boss is the worst! He gives me triple the work that one person could do and I can't take it. I feel horrible everyday after work and I can't do this much longer.
  - Powerful: My boss has very high expectations of those on his team. He gives us a lot of work and may not realize that it's more than we can handle in a 40 hour workweek. It's starting to affect my mental health. I have a few choices:
    - Do the work and feel frazzled, anxious and overworked. If I choose this, I can't complain about it all of the time. I'm choosing it.
    - Create boundaries and only do what I can fit into a 40 hour work week, since that's what I'm getting paid for and what I've agreed to do according to my salary (I make $x per year in exchange for 40 hours of work per week). Stick to my boundaries.
    - Talk to the upper management about my dilemma and need for less on my plate in order to do my job well
    - Find a new job that prioritizes work/life balance and meets the other criteria I'm looking for.

- Life keeps delivering blow after blow.
  - Victim: Literally, every day continues to get worse. Everyone around me is out to get me. I can't imagine what else could happen and will happen tomorrow.
  - Powerful: Life is throwing me a lot of challenges right now. I'm thankful I'm resilient and have a support system to help me right now.

- Your home catches on fire.
  - Victim: Everything is gone. I'll never get it back. God is literally throwing fire on me, he hates me so much. Stop smiting me. How could things get worse? (PS don't ever ask this question - the Universe will answer you).
  - Powerful: I'm not sure how this is serving me in this moment, but I know that eventually I'll see how this supported me in some way.

- You unexpectedly get laid off from your job.
  - Victim: No job ever works out for me! Nothing in life works for me! Why is everyone always out to get me?
  - Powerful: Maybe this is a sign to finally move forward with my side hustle full-time! Maybe the Universe is just forcing me out of this job because I didn't really enjoy how I was spending my days. Thank you for the nudge, Universe. I know I will figure this out.

We all have challenging things that happen in life - and it's ok for us to vent and complain about something occasionally. When really tough things happen, we are allowed to experience our emotions about it. That's called being human. The trick is not getting stuck in Victimville. When we are in that space, we are in a lower vibration and want to shift out of it quickly! It's when this becomes our permanent lens on life that it becomes disastrous and we begin to attract from that place. We want to attract ABUNDANCE - not more of the victim-y events.

Where in your life are you choosing to view things from a victim perspective? List at least 3 ways.

How could you view these situations as happening FOR you?

What magic could actually come from these circumstances? How could this actually be a huge blessing?

Who can help keep you accountable to viewing life through a Powerful Perspective? This could be a spouse, friend, alarm that pops up on your phone saying "remember to view things powerfully", or a friendly post-it note reminder on your bathroom mirror.

ENERGY HEALING: FILLING UP THE ROOT CHAKRA

It's so easy in today's world to become ungrounded with the amount of activity and chaos in our daily lives and the large amount of energy we come into contact with on a daily basis. Coming to a practice of grounding ourselves with Mother Earth's energy is vital. The practices below are some of my favorites to keep myself grounded and centered. We can find ourselves ungrounded daily, so don't be afraid to utilize these support tools on a daily basis (or a few times per day, if needed)!

Visualization:

Sit down in a comfortable position, either seated or connected to the Earth with your feet firmly on the ground. Breathe deeply for a few minutes and come to peace within your body. Feel the stillness move throughout you.

Close your eyes and imagine yourself as a big, beautiful tree that climbs high into the sky. Feel your spine straighten as you embody this tree, standing confidently and tall.

Bring your attention to your feet, feeling all four corners of your feet and begin to imagine that just like this tall tree, you too, have roots extending down into the Earth, deeper and deeper. Your roots reach all the way into the center of the Earth, where they recharge from Mother Earth's energy.

Allow yourself to release any heavy energy, negative energy or energy you are holding for others into the Earth through these roots. Ask "please transmute these negative energies and return to me energized and revitalized energy." Mother Earth will recycle these energies for you and transmute the negativity. Imagine feeling a beautiful white light move upwards through your roots, until it's reached the bottom of your feet and it moves throughout your body. Feel this powerful energy and notice how it feels as it activates in your body.

Physical Tools and Support:

- Create a practice of "Earthing" – standing barefoot or sitting in nature, whether it is in the grass, soil or sand. This helps to release heavy and dense energy and realign with Mother Earth's energy.
- Spend more time in nature, in general!
- Bring green plants into your home.
- Utilize Himalayan salt lamps to balance the ions emitted by all of the electronics in your home. These lamps have a lot of other health benefits as well and help to purify the air around them.
- Place EMF protection products near your electronics.
- Wear more earthy colors and root colors, like dark green, brown and deep red.

- Eat grounding foods, such as root vegetables.
- Jump up and down or stomp your feet.

Root Chakra Affirmations:

- I am safe and protected in my body and in my home.
- I am nourished and deeply supported.
- I am taken care of and provided for by The Universe.
- I am grounded and calm.
- All of my needs are always met.
- I belong here.

Root Chakra Crystals:

- Shungite, black obsidian or black tourmaline for protection
- Hematite for grounding
- Red Jasper for earth connection
- Bloodstone for patience
- Smoky Quartz to let go of the past

Root Chakra Essential Oils:

When you purchase essential oils, make sure that you've done your research. These companies are not regulated and can claim just about anything in their packaging. I prefer DoTerra or YoungLiving oils as I find them to be the highest quality, at the time I'm writing this. The only mid-level oil I use occasionally is Kate's Magick or Aura Cacia. If you're ingesting the oils, though, you must use a higher quality oil. If you need help purchasing, you can always order DoTerra oils through me on my website for wholesale pricing.

For grounding, you can put oil on your feet and hands! When I put it on my feet, I'll usually put socks on afterwards or give it a few minutes to soak in so that I don't slip and slide all over the floor. :)

- Cypress for connecting to grounded tree energy.
- Cedarwood for grounded energy.
- Sandalwood for peaceful and tranquil grounding.
- Myrrh for connection to Mother Earth.
- DoTerra has a great oil called "Balance" that is my favorite grounding oil as well as another oil called "Steady" that works very well.

Sacral Chakra

Svādhiṣṭhāna

Sacral Chakra

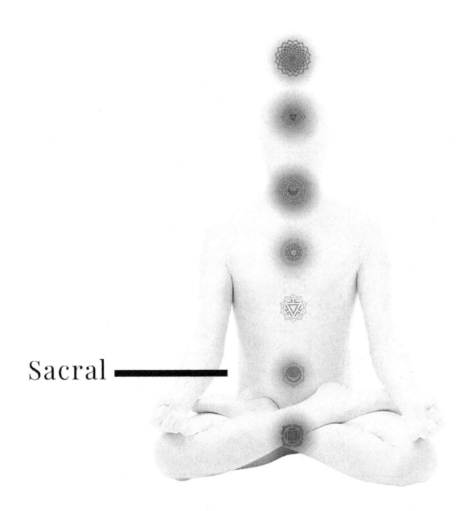

Sacral ————

SACRAL CHAKRA: SVADHISTHANA

The Sacral Chakra energetically governs our creativity, confidence, pleasure, vitality and expression of our sexuality. It's our center of personal expression of our passions. Physically, it's located about 3 inches below the belly button, right around the pubic bone, and is normally represented by the color orange. When the Sacral Chakra is blocked, it's challenging to feel excited about life and may feel like your life is lacking passion.

This is a chakra that can hold a lot of trauma - we're going to be doing a lot of energetic clean up here that may make you feel uncomfortable, blush a little or want to grab a glass of wine. If there is any area of this book that you want to skip, it will probably be this one. Remember your commitment you made to show up fully for yourself! The work we want to skip is usually what we need most. Don't avoid it, especially if it is confronting.

The Sacral Chakra holds so much magic and it is an area most of us have a lot of dust and cobwebs covering up all of our passion, joy and excitement for life. Some of the work we do here may seem like it doesn't relate to money and abundance, but trust me, it does. This energetic work will support enhanced vitality in many ways as well as amplifying your relationship with money and abundance!

We are covering so many big topics in this section - really pay attention to which areas you feel you have room to grow and expand in. Each of these principles could become years of deep study and practice to embody - we are just tapping in to see where you're at with each of them and what's not being fully expressed within you.

Treat your money as if you were in a relationship with it.

#SacredWealth

ABUNDANCE PRINCIPLE 8: RING IT ALL OUT

The most important thing to understand about money is that we are in a relationship with it. When we imagine money as a relationship, it gives us a whole new perspective. If you treated your best friends the way that you treat money, what would they do? Most of us have only seen money as a physical entity - an obligation or something that we *have* to deal with. Most people also allow money to completely control their life and decisions. If your romantic partner treated you that way, would you still want to be in that partnership?

Much of our work in this area is about upgrading our relationship with money so that it feels loved, appreciated, nourished and understood. With the education we've received regarding money, this probably seems so silly! Remember how I told you to keep an open mind? Be open to the idea that creating a stronger relationship with money will help you create powerful results and manifestations.

Today's effort is one of the most powerful activities you can do in terms of clearing your energy around money. Imagine your feelings about money as a heavy, wet, dripping rag. The water inside this rag represents all of your pent up thoughts and feelings about money. Imagine trying to clean your countertop with a rag like this - you'd be spreading gross bacteria (your low vibrational and stale beliefs) all over the countertop. Ew.

We must release this heaviness to bring in anything new. To do so, we are going to write a letter to money. This exercise can be incredibly insightful and has facilitated so many massive transformations. Don't rush through this. Take your time and make sure you have privacy. Money is often incredibly emotional for us to work with and we have to be able to release those heavier emotions in privacy so that we feel completely safe and don't hold back at all. Our feelings about money usually correlate to much deeper beliefs, so do not be surprised if more comes up than you are expecting.

Step 1: Take a moment of stillness. Clear your mind of whatever has happened earlier today. Give yourself a few minutes to just breathe and get quiet.

Step 2: Start writing "Dear Money." Follow up with any emotion you have. EVERYTHING is allowed in this letter. You don't have to know what you are going to say - just write whatever comes out of you. Whatever comes out is perfect. As you complete writing, keep asking yourself "what else?" Get it all out. Space is provided below, but feel free to write on another sheet of paper if you'd like more room to express yourself. .

Step 3: Close out your letter discussing what you'd like your relationship with money to be like in the future.

A few questions to help get your energy moving:
- What do you feel when you think about money?
- What's your history with money?
- Do you feel supported by money?
- Are you happy with how money is showing up in your life?
- What is the primary emotion you feel in regards to money?
- If you received a million dollars right now, how would you feel?
- Do you like spending money? Making money? Saving money? Investing?

A few prompts to support you:
- What is the relationship you want with money?
- How do you want her to show up for you?
- How would it look ideally to you?
- Acknowledge her. Let her know what you are thankful for regarding money.
- Ask her to give you signs about how you can work with money more effectively.

Write Your Letter to Money

I write letters to money a few times per year. It's such a beautiful way to check in with where you're at and release anything that is weighing you down. The really interesting part is keeping these letters and seeing how the dynamic shifts over the years!

You've now written your letter to money, and you're going to switch seats and write a letter back to yourself. If money had a message for you, what would it be? **Don't overthink this.** Even if the message doesn't come immediately, set the intention to get a sign from money with a message at the perfect Divine timing.

If money had a message for you, what would it be?

"There are no small upsets. They are all equally disturbing to our peace of mind."

A COURSE IN MIRACLES

#SacredWealth

ABUNDANCE PRINCIPLE 9: CLEAR OUT THE TRAUMA

Trauma lives in our body when we don't address it and repress the emotions. Most of us were literally taught how to stuff down our emotions, rather than feel them. Do you notice how babies and toddlers openly feel their feelings and it's accepted? At a certain age, this stops being "accepted" and you may start to receive comments to make sure you know your expression makes others uncomfortable. Do any of these phrases below sound familiar to you?

Traumas, big or small, impact us deeply. We know the big traumas in our life, but we often overlook the small things that made a big impact on us, as if they aren't large enough to cause any damage. Here are a few examples of small traumas from my personal life that I thought of in 30 seconds:

- The kid who told me I had buck teeth in front of my crush at 13 years old and I was mortified, thinking that now my whole future with this dweeb was ruined now that my big secret had been revealed (as if he couldn't see them himself. I definitely had buck teeth). *cues J.Cole song up "Crooked Smile"*
- Friends gossiping behind my back about me, but being nice to my face and pretending they were genuine friends. Hello, trust issues.
- Being taller than literally all of the boys in my class until high school, and being reminded of it every 3.2 seconds. Hello, bad posture and confidence issues. Also PSA... we shouldn't be commenting on anyone's height. No one likes it. You wouldn't tell a short person "wow, you are so miniature, just like a leprechaun" so don't tell tall girls

"wow, you are so tall!" Like we don't already know. Thanks for revealing an ancient secret of life, Gertrude. You just blew my world wide open. How will I approach life from now on, knowing this hidden wisdom? Ok, I'll stop.

- Individuals constantly reminding me that I was "too much" for expressing myself authentically or "too intense."
- People I trusted letting me down, over and over again and manipulating me.
- Feeling smothered, micromanaged and overprotected.
- Shame and guilt from decisions that did not reflect my true Divinity.
- Feeling abandoned or rejected in "small" (and large) ways.

These seem tiny and I purposefully made them laugh-able, but it gives you an idea of how seemingly small traumas can be - we could all write a list 500 items deep. It's necessary to go there because we want to be CLEAN and SPARKLY on the inside, not muddy with old memories that we're stuffing down. We aren't the judge of what's "big" or "small" trauma - we just know it's gotta go! The "small" traumas can take less time to let go of and help train us to learn how we can release the big ones. Don't discount anything that hurt you.

List out at least 20 of the Traumas that have affected you most in your life. Think through your life from childhood to the present day and what is affecting you most on a daily basis (or what comes to mind first).

1.

2.

3.

4.

5.

6.

7.

8.

9.

10.

11.

12.

13.

14.

15.

16.

17.

18.

19.

20.

When we bring these traumas up to the surface, a lot can happen. Really tune into these feelings and emotions and let yourself FEEL them. When we say "oh, I need to go wash the dishes" to conveniently ignore our feelings, we're doing ourselves a massive disservice. Journaling is my favorite way to move through heavy emotions, along with moving my body, screaming into a pillow (I'm not joking - this is extremely healing for our throat chakra), and deep breathing through Lion's Breath exercises!

A few weeks ago, I was upset about something small, but the emotions around it were BIG. I recognized that if I didn't move my energy, I'd 100% lash out at the people around me. I journaled, which didn't help enough, as I still felt the fumes inside and I didn't want to shapeshift into my dragon energy with the people I was with, so I decided to go for a walk. I dramatically grabbed my phone, headphone and keys (probably slamming the door behind me) and began the intense power walk, listening to music that helped me really get into my terrifying emotions. This supported me through deeply feeling what I was feeling with honesty.

When we try to diminish the feelings, we're doing ourselves a disservice. The first thing we have to do is be honest about what we are feeling! So just imagine me, walking on the beach alone, at an extremely fast pace like I have an appointment to go murder someone , with a fire ablaze in the background as I take each step, definitely listening to Beyonce "Who the f*ck do you think I is?" I walked out that heavy, fierce, dragon-y energy out for 2 hours until it released and I felt like a normal calm version of myself again.

Unlike what doctors and our medical system would tell us , dis-ease is formed from emotional repression. There are so many studies that show people with cancer who do the work to heal themselves EMOTIONALLY have a much higher rate of recovery.

So, consider this doing work for your health and well-being. I share many other tips to move through shadow work on my social media pages, so make sure to follow me there if you want more support around healing work (@aly.wilkins on Instagram).

Do you allow yourself to FEEL your emotions? What does that normally look like for you? (a quick cry? Sleeping for 6 days? Rageful journaling? Taking it out on someone else?)

What's the most common emotion you feel when hard things come up? (Anger, Sadness, Depression, Anxiety, Rage, Shame, Guilt, Numbness, etc)

What were you taught about emotions and being sensitive growing up?

How did your parents (or whoever raised you) handle their emotions?

Which memory is bringing up the most emotion for you right now?

Give yourself 20 minutes minimum and journal about this memory. Let it all out. Ring it all out. This isn't about being a Positive Polly, it's about letting all your emotions flood out onto your paper. I will provide space below, but I recommend you write this on a separate sheet of paper and then when you are complete, either shred it or (safely) burn it so the energy can be released.

PS - our most "significant" traumas will likely not go away overnight - they do take awareness and consistent re-parenting of ourselves to fully move through. I cannot tell you the number of times I've said "Omg haven't I moved through this already?!" Sometimes the first time is the charm, and sometimes the 72nd time's the charm.

Revisit the rest of the items on this list and complete this exercise as you have space and time. You don't have to do this all at once - emotional work is deep and takes a significant amount of energy. Take this at the pace you feel intuitively guided to move through it.

"You can't run out of creativity. The more creative energy you use, the more you'll have."

MAYA ANGELOU

#SacredWealth

ABUNDANCE PRINCIPLE 10: TUNE INTO YOUR CREATIVITY

When I first started energy work - the first place that was very clear needed work was my Sacral Chakra. I felt so blocked but worse off, I was so BORED with life. Lack of creativity in our life creates chronic boredom.... You know the routine - go to work, come home, feed yourself and your family, chill out for an hour, go to sleep and repeat the same thing. Where is the fun in that?

We usually think of creativity only pertaining to artists or someone incredibly talented with music, painting, singing, etc. The thing is... we were told a big lie. We are all constantly creating something - whether it's a bad vibration in the room as we complain about how many times we stubbed our toe this week, or creating magical energy through our vibrant gratitude.

I'm not asking you to go become Picasso overnight - I want to ask you to tune into what excites you creatively so you can start tapping into that more often. We are all incredibly creative, most of us have just been raised not to tap into it. Creativity is one of the parts of life that makes it the most enjoyable! If we can't express ourselves, literally what is the point? We aren't built to be robots living in a system and repeating the same 14 tasks over and over everyday. We each have unique expressions that help make the world a more beautiful, loving and exciting place to be. Some of those expressions are from our God-given gifts or personality, but many change daily with our mood and inspirations that flow to us!

So, time to tune in.

When you think of creativity, what comes to mind?

Do you think of yourself as being creative?

When you have done "creative" things in the past, what would that look like?

Do you give yourself any time to tap into your creativity? If so, what does that look like?

Is there anything you've been wanting to do, but haven't?

My challenge for you this week is to do something creative that feels exciting. I suggest putting this on your calendar so that you actually do it! This is by no means a complete list - but these are some of my favorite ways to tap into my creativity :

- Elemental Dance (we do this at every retreat I host! If you live in a big city, there are many places you can go to experience this kind of dance. It's incredibly freeing.)
- Doing artwork of any kind - painting, drawing, sculpting
- Making handmade jewelry
- Playing a musical instrument
- Putting together really beautiful outfits that make you feel fierce
- Cooking beautiful meals
- Creating sacred spaces and ceremonies
- Organizing your crystals around the house to create certain vibrations in each area
- Having fun with interior design
- When I was younger, I consistently made handmade cards and would spend literally hours per card, using intricate stamps and coloring each one, like it was my life's work
- Making crystal candles, sage bundles, essential oil blends and other healing tools
- Singing and dancing to your favorite music
- Coloring!
- Making handmade gifts with love and intention

Do you see how endless this list could be (and how fun)?! Most "projects" you work on are actually creative projects! You can source creativity into literally everything you do - from pouring your water, to cooking your meals each night, to creating a scrapbook or photo album.

What's something creative you will commit to doing this week?

Once you've had fun tuning into your creative energy, come back to this page.

How did it feel to express your creativity?

Was it easy for you? Did it take a while to experience it?

Creativity comes easily to us - but many of us have also been programmed that creativity is girly or a waste of time or not productive... so we may have some resistance. I wanted to address it here because this is actually very normal! Keep adding it in your calendar and you'll get more and more comfortable expressing this side of yourself. Life without creativity is just boring.

"Part of being an empowered human is being in touch with your own sexuality, and sexual power."

REGINA THOMASHAUER

#SacredWealth

ABUNDANCE PRINCIPLE 11: EXPAND YOUR EXPERIENCE OF SEXUALITY + INTIMACY

Sexuality is so aligned with our creative energy. Think about it... sex is literally creating a human out of thin air. A woman birthing a child is the epitome of creation. The Root Chakra has a lot of sexual elements to it - as it relates to everything survival based, and sexuality is how we create another generation that allows the human race to continue.

However, the Sacral Chakra I believe holds most of our trauma around sex itself, our sexual experiences and our sexual expression - so we're going in deep in this area today. Being able to express ourselves sexually and experience pleasure in this way is such a huge component of life that society has taught us to suppress and see as dirty or unacceptable. Think about how women are basically categorized as virgins or whores, with no in between, while men can pretty much do whatever they want without judgment. This principle will start to open you up to see how you are owning or hiding your sexuality, and hopefully give you some spaces to look at to see where you can express yourself more fully.

This topic alone could be a series of 28 books, so know that this work goes very deep and we are just skimming the surface with today's activity. When answering the following questions, write whatever comes to mind first without thinking too much about it.

When you think about sex, what comes to mind?

What did you learn about sex as a child? Did your parents talk to you about it? Were they open? Were they shut down?

How did your parents react to your sexuality? How do they react to sexuality in general?

What was your first sexual experience like? How did it impact you?

What was your first truly enjoyable sexual experience like?

What was (one of) your most fun sexual experiences like?

TRIGGER WARNING - Approach with caution and sensitivity.

Unfortunately, a high percentage of people have experienced sexual abuse of some sort in their lifetime. This shapes our beliefs and feelings about sex dramatically. If you are in the percentage of people who have not experienced this, you have still likely experienced some form of pain when it comes to sex. Just like the traumas we discussed earlier, there is no comparison between a "big" or "small" trauma. Do not discount anything that hurts you.

What was your most painful sexual experience like? Have you suppressed that memory or worked through it already? How did it impact you and your daily life? How does this still impact your life today?

Breathe. Take a deep breath. Sex is one of the most intimate parts of our life - and we talk about it the least. It impacts our emotions and our vibration so heavily. Most of us have some form of trauma around sex and it is incredibly necessary for us to dive in deeper in this area so that we can clear that trauma and make room for more beautiful energy.

What is your relationship with your sexuality right now? Open? Closed off? Awkward? Overactive? Frustrated? Afraid of intimacy? Addicted?

What are you pretending not to know about your sexuality?

Do you feel guilty or shameful when it comes to sex or what your preferences are? Why?

What do you want more of sexually?

What makes you feel excited sexually?

How do you feel about self-pleasure?

Where do you feel stifled or smothered sexually?

Rate your sex life 0-10. Why did you rate it that way? (PS - You don't need a partner to have a sex life).

Do you feel sexy? Why or why not? What "makes someone sexy?"

PS - you are super sexy. Whatever you wrote above, if it indicated you weren't, is inaccurate.

This will likely bring up a lot. Take a few moments to write out anything that may be coming up for you from these prompts.

Here are some wonderful books that can support you with diving deeper into sexual trauma, sacred sexuality and understanding more about sex in general. What most of us are taught about sex is that it is purely physical - and that's just not true. It can be so much more than that, if you want it to be! In addition to these titles, finding someone you trust to talk to is invaluable, such as a therapist, a life coach or someone trained in somatic healing work.

Come As You Are   She Comes First   Finding God Through Sex
Pussy : A Reclamation   Sex for One   Women's Anatomy of Arousal
Waking the Tiger   Sexual Healing Journey   Kama Sutra

Sex is a highly loaded topic that has so much conditioning around it. Notice any beliefs that come up for you around sexuality and go back to Principle 2 in the Root Chakra section to determine if these beliefs are helping you or hurting you.

LET INTIMACY + SENSUALITY IN

Many of us shy away from our sensuality and intimacy, as we may be afraid of letting people truly see us. We cover ourselves with a variety of masks so that we will be accepted by others and to avoid rejection or pain. Intimacy requires that we remove those masks and be brave enough to let others really see us as we truly are. As we open ourselves, we open to experiencing so many new levels of love, joy and passion.

For a moment, let's reframe what sensuality means. When we think of that word, usually the mind may go straight to imagining wearing sexy lingerie with a room filled with candles for a romantic night. Often, we associate sensuality and intimacy only with our sex lives, but our whole life can be a ceremony of sensuality! Intimacy is much more than just showing our sensuality in the bedroom. Being truly intimate is sharing yourself in your most vulnerable states and truly connecting, with yourself, or with someone else. When we bring intimacy and sensuality into our everyday life, it looks like truly slowing down and enjoying life as a sacred ceremony.

I'd like you to shift how you view sensuality so you can truly see it as a way of living - a way that we interact with the world on a daily basis. Today's work will be a practice of seeing where you can bring more intimacy and sensuality into the small moments of your day.

What does intimacy mean to you?

When do you feel most intimate? When have you felt most intimate in the past?

Who do you feel most comfortable being intimate around? (Be honest here if you don't feel comfortable being vulnerable with anyone quite yet).

Sexual intimacy comes easily for some and for others, it feels excruciatingly vulnerable to open ourselves in such a way. How comfortable are you with intimacy sexually?

Do you feel like you can be your authentic self with others? Do the people closest to you really know you?

What areas are you less comfortable being intimate in? What's off limits? Is there anything you wouldn't share with others? Does this vary based on the person?

On a scale of 1-10, how well would you say you know yourself and are intimate with who you really are?

If you're having trouble allowing yourself to be vulnerable and intimate with others, start with yourself.

How Do Your Clothes Make You Feel?

What we wear impacts how we feel! I know I feel a lot more sensual when I'm wearing a beautiful, lacy top versus wearing a raggedy sweatshirt from 14 years ago with a chocolate stain on it. It's not that we can't have more casual clothes - it's just that we want to be more intentional with what we buy in the first place - and what we hold on to.

What clothing makes you feel most sensual?

How do you feel when you wear these items?

Look at your closet. What are the majority of the clothes you own? Consider colors and types of clothing.

How could you create more sensuality in your wardrobe? Do you feel sexier in certain materials? Do you feel more joy in certain styles or colors?

Personally, I have a rule that I only purchase clothes (anything, really) if it is a 10/10. It's way too easy to end up with a closet of 7/10's if you buy everything you like in the moment at Target on your shopping trip to get coffee creamer.

Let's Look at Your Eating Habits

Eating is something that we do every single day and an area we can easily introduce more sensuality. This doesn't mean you have to be a vixen, seductively eating your popsicle in slow motion and making every head turn.... but it could! The purpose of these questions is to take inventory of where you can introduce more intimacy - not to judge yourself or try to become anything other than "what you are." This is just to note where you can slow things down and truly enjoy the little things.

How quickly do you normally eat your food? Are certain meals rushed? Do you enjoy eating your meals, or are you shoveling them down quickly?

Do you genuinely taste your food when you eat it? Often, we are multi-tasking when we eat. Even if you are watching television while you eat dinner or even just talking to someone, are you really tuning into how your food tastes?

How often do you multitask while eating your food? Cramming your lunch meal in at work in front of your computer, while you're on a Zoom meeting and are stapling papers together at the same time? Would it even be possible to enjoy your food while doing so many things?

In what kind of environment do you eat your meals in?

A few ideas to expand your eating experience :

- Slow down the process significantly. Challenge yourself to take as long as you can with each bite and really take in the flavors, textures and smells of your food.
- Expand your senses - what does your food smell like? Feel like? Taste like? Look like? Really take a few moments to just observe.
- Create a more intimate environment while you're eating! Instead of eating at the same picnic bench on your lunch break, maybe you can bring a blanket and sit in the grass. Maybe you can light a candle while you eat your dinner. What could you do to enhance your dining experience?
- Add a little extra pizzazz - maybe it's just adding a basil leaf to the top of your spaghetti. Or adding a sliced lemon on the side of your water cup. It doesn't seem like much, but this really adds pleasure into your dining experience!
- Stretch yourself if you'd like to eat something seductively! Tasting mango juice dripping is a pleasure we often don't experience when we rush through it or focus our thoughts on avoiding a mess.

Does Eye Contact Scare You?

We'll talk more about the act of receiving later in the book, but we'll touch on one element here : Eye Contact. Eye contact is highly intimate - and you'll notice if you try to keep eye contact with most people, they will look away.

People say that "the eyes are the windows to the Soul." So - when we are comfortable holding eye contact with others, it usually showcases our comfort with ourselves and our level of confidence. Trauma can also deeply affect our willingness to hold eye contact - it's a measure of faux safety to not allow ourselves to connect on that level. If you see others unable to keep their eye contact with you - or you, yourself have trouble with holding your gaze - be loving and gentle. We never know what others are going through at the moment.

In multiple retreats I've held, I have the retreat attendees pair up and take 10 minutes to literally stare into the eyes of their partner. No talking - just eye gazing. At the end of this exercise, usually the partners feel much closer to one another and feel they know each other on a deeper level - or even see a mirror reflection of themselves. Occasionally, someone will not be able to let the other in, and even without talking to the other person, the partner will say that they felt the person was distant. I've done this with others as well in many retreats and have experienced wild energy exchanges! *Eye contact is magical* - don't let the initial hesitancy of letting someone in scare you off!

Chances are, if you ask your office buddy, Carl, to eye gaze with you for 10 minutes - it's going to be a hard no. However, you can hold your eye contact with him 5 seconds longer! Doing this with your significant other will definitely deepen your bond. Highly recommended!

Where do you fall within this? Is holding eye contact difficult for you?

```
[                                                                    ]
```

Challenge yourself to hold your eye contact 5% longer! If you continue this practice, you'll likely notice an increase in self-confidence and feeling more powerful! People will also feel like they can trust you more. Avoiding eye contact is usually something we do when we aren't truly connecting with someone (or if we are lying)!

Slowing Down Your Pace

When we are constantly rushing throughout our days, it's going to be difficult to be intimate with anything or anyone. We simply aren't moving slowly enough to do so.

How often are you rushing through your days? Is there a particular part of your day that feels more rushed than other parts?

```
[                                                                    ]
```

What could help support you to slow down in your day? Can you request help from someone? Do you need a reminder? Would preparation or planning of some kind support you in creating more space during your day?

```
[                                                                    ]
```

What moments of your day would be most impactful for you to slow down for?

```
[                                                                    ]
```

Sensuality Has a Special Place in Expressing Our Sexuality

Is your experience of making love usually very fast? Or do you allow yourself to take things at a slower pace?

In what areas do you notice that you hold back intimately?

What scares you sexually in terms of intimacy?

Do you shy away from eye contact during sex?

Where do you not allow someone fully in during a sexual experience?

Challenge yourself to stretch yourself here! When we are playing small or holding back in any area, we aren't experiencing what's truly possible

A few additional thoughts to expand the possibilities of intimacy in our daily lives:

- If you pass a beautiful flower, do you notice it? Do you take 1 minute to truly revel in its beauty and smell it's fragrance?
- Are you actually experiencing the "noteworthy" moments of your life? Or just recording it for your social media feed?
- When you put your moisturizer on before bed, are you slapping it on your face as quickly as possible? Let's take the moment to appreciate our skin as well as our moisturizer and the ability to slowly massage it into our face, with love.
- When was the last time you witnessed a sunrise or sunset?

Taking the time to create more sacred ceremonies in our daily moments is easy - it's just something we get to become more aware of so we can expand our pleasure and joy in each moment.

Your deepest desires
are a part of your
purpose and mission
on Earth. They are in
no way random.

#SacredWealth

ABUNDANCE PRINCIPLE 12: CELEBRATE YOUR TRUE DESIRES

I have been told more times than I can count *"you can't have everything you want, it's just too much."* There is nothing more Soul-Crushing than that phrase. That phrase made me depressed for years, sitting in my average job, crying in the bathroom at work wondering how I could do this "working a 9-5" thing for another 50 years and ignore my big dreams that felt so non-negotiable to me.

We get to operate life from a place of "ALL NEEDS MET" - if you're reading this book, that means you had extra money to buy a book, or the Universe found a way for it to get into your hands. Many people in the world would give anything for that. I've had multiple messages from people asking me to send them a book because they can't afford it and don't have a library or any books at their disposal. If you're reading this, you likely live in the US or North America and have access to pretty much anything you need. All of your needs are met.

However; that doesn't mean we just settle for the average white picket fence life of mediocrity just because that's what most people do.

Before I was 24, I never really dreamed of anything other than having a good job that paid well. That's what I was taught was the dream. "Get a good job at a big company that will take care of you and you'll live happily ever after." When I did that, I quickly became incredibly miserable. I didn't care about the work I was doing - it didn't mean anything to me. I didn't care about the companies that employed me - they weren't creating any kind of impact that felt important to me. My soul was not fulfilled - in fact, it was being drained more, and more, by the day.

Then, a miracle happened. I caught a glimpse of a couple I knew that were only a few years older than me who were living their dreams, working for themselves and feeling absolutely fulfilled. I started watching them and finding more people living life on their terms - and before I knew it, I had quit my job with a plan to go to Bali and do yoga teacher training. It was really just running away from my problems, but it was what I needed at the time. It was the seed that planted my entire life now - and the life I'm creating for the future.

From there, my world opened up immensely and I began to see so many possibilities. I started to recognize that my desires were there for a reason and that they were implanted in me when I was created. They were not me "wanting too much." They were a part of my purpose on Earth.

> *"When are you going to realize that being normal is not necessarily a virtue? It rather denotes a lack of courage."* - Alice Hoffman

What are your deep desires? What do you want in your life?

Is there any guilt or shame attached to that? Where do you think that might come from?

Do you think it's possible to receive those desires?

Do you know anyone else who has accomplished that? (If not, find them).

If you knew you would be 1000% supported and could not fail, what would you desire?

List 20 BIG desires you'd like to call into your life.

1.

2.

3.

4.

5.

6.

7.

8.

9.

10.

11.

12.

13.

14.

15.

16.

17.

18.

19.

20.

Here are 5 of my big desires - take a look at your list and see if you can go even BIGGER.

1. Massive career as an author with impactful books - I imagine writing more than 30 books in my lifetime that I'm crazy proud of, that are translated into several different languages and have many matching oracle decks. Most importantly, creating works of art that live on far beyond my time and remain impactful decade after decade. In the short term, I see myself adding emails and letters to a big, overflowing box filled with notes from readers that are sharing how my work has impacted their life in miraculous ways.

2. One day, I will go on a world cruise for 6 months to a year with my partner! It would be a luxury cruise and we would have the best room on the boat, naturally, with the most amazing view and a big bathtub next to the balcony. Also, a fireplace, because why not.

3. Create massive impact in the rainforest to help stop rainforest deforestation, conserve the land, protect the indigenous peoples who still live there and all of the animal species that thrive in the rainforest. I don't know what this looks like right now, but I know clarity will come at the right time. I envision having a team of amazing humans who help support me with this and are just as passionate about it as I am.

4. Be sponsored by Rainforest Alliance Certified luxury hotels and airlines. Travel is my favorite activity, so why not get paid for the reviews I would share anyway? :)

5. Travel across the country and the world with my future partner and (maybe) babies, sort of like the Wild Thornberries (anyone remember that old Nickelodeon show? It was my fave as a kid!). Traveling the world, experiencing many cultures and sharing energy healing and motivational work across the globe, learning from the best of the best. Additionally, bringing my parents, sister and her family and my partner's family with us on some of these trips to create amazing family memories.

ENERGY HEALING: FILLING UP THE SACRAL CHAKRA

The Sacral Chakra is an incredibly magical area as we are birthing from this area - birthing literal babies, creative projects, passion, enthusiasm, etc into the world. When the Sacral Chakra is in balance, we are feeling creative, passionate, sensual and excited about life. That being said, this is also a highly sensitive area as most of us hold a lot of trauma here. Women, particularly, hold a lot of trauma in our wombs that can even be passed down from our lineage. This is important work to do and the first area I personally started healing within myself. Since then, I've come back for many more rounds of clearing and the tools below are what have supported me most in my healing.

Visualization:

Take a few moments to get comfortable, taking slow and deep breaths. Perhaps dimming the lights or lighting a candle to create sacred space. Place one hand on your Sacral Chakra area, a few inches below your belly button. Breathe into this space.

Imagine placing a red rose within this area and watch it slowly bloom open, radiating golden healing light from within the rose. This golden light moves throughout your womb area, completely filling every cell with beautiful healing energy. See the rose start to spin, knowing that as it spins, it is moving and circulating this healing energy throughout this creative space. How quickly is it spinning? Does it slow down in certain areas? Are some areas a little stickier to move through? Notice that as this rose spins within your Sacral Chakra, it is clearing out all dense, dusty, heavy energy. Allow the rose to spin as long as it feels right for you. When you feel complete, place both hands now on your womb area and say "Thank you for healing this Sacred Space in my body."

Physical Tools and Support:

- Taking a healing bath with roses or other flower petals, using the oils mentioned below for aromatherapy. The Sacral Center is very connected to water, so spending time in any kind of water (oceans, showers, bathtubs, rivers) will be healing.
- For women, yoni steams or yoni eggs to heal your energy and cleanse the Sacral area.
- Reiki healing is a really powerful modality in general, but this area can hold a lot of trauma so reiki healing supports moving the energy in a deeper way.
- Wearing more orange clothing and underwear.
- Eating more orange foods, like carrots, oranges, turmeric, pumpkin, butternut squash, mango, cantaloupe, orange bell peppers and sweet potatoes.
- Getting into your creativity and expressing your artistic self.
- Creating a journaling practice to work through emotions and traumas.

Sacral Chakra Affirmations:

- It is safe for me to express my sensuality.
- I am confident in who I am.
- I allow my creativity to flow through me freely.
- I embrace and celebrate my sexuality.
- I live a passionate and pleasurable life.
- I am loveable and desirable.
- I enjoy pleasure in all areas of my life.
- I am comfortable in my body.

Sacral Chakra Crystal:

Carnelian is my top choice for Sacral Chakra healing. This stone is specifically for creativity, sensuality, confidence and energy. I recommend purchasing several pieces of this from your local metaphysical shop or Etsy. When I was working on healing this area intensely, I had carnelian bracelets I would wear and would also keep a big stone on my desk at work, on my nightstand, and would even put smaller crystals in my bra or in my pockets! You can also put the crystal in your pillowcase, but just test it out because sometimes carnelian can give you a lot of energy as well and may cause difficulty sleeping.

Other crystals that are supportive here are sunstone, amber and moonstone.

Sacral Chakra Essential Oils:

Place these oils directly on the Sacral Chakra! As always, you may need to use a carrier oil (like coconut oil) with the essential oil if your skin is sensitive.

- Ylang Ylang for hormonal balancing and sensuality.
- Cardamom for an underactive sacral chakra.
- Jasmine for sensuality and feminine energy.
- Rose for divine feminine energy and healing.
- Clary Sage for calming and clearing.

Solar Plexus Chakra

Maṇipūra

Solar Plexus Chakra

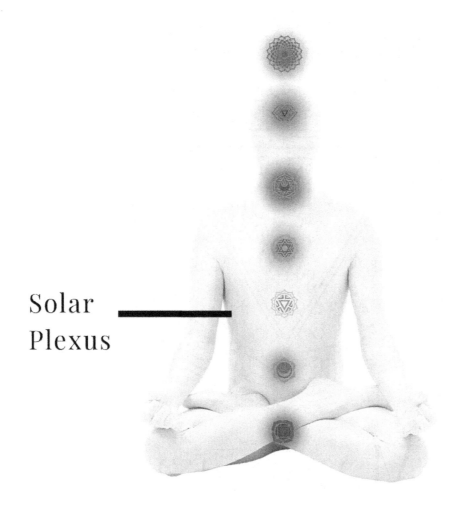

Solar
Plexus

SOLAR PLEXUS : MANIPURA

Have you ever come across someone who just absolutely radiates? They light up the whole room with their presence. This person has a very healthy Solar Plexus chakra (and self-esteem). Our Solar Plexus Chakra is located right at the belly button and is a highly important space to heal as it is our place of power - where our true inner light shines from.

When we feel empowered, confident and valuable, our solar plexus is balanced. Think about the artist Rihanna - she confidently shines her light and does not dim for anyone. It is apparent that she believes in herself and treats herself in the Highest, because she values herself.

When we feel a lack of confidence in ourselves and experience low self-esteem, a rebalancing is needed. Unfortunately, our society almost encourages that we dim this light, so almost none of us are shining at our fullest potential. Many of us suffer from symptoms of disempowerment that we have learned or allowed to come into our space that we will dive into in this chapter.

The work we are doing here will help to recognize where you are dimming your shine and support you in dialing up the amount of light that you radiate in the world. You'll learn how to operate in your full brightness and how to protect yourself from people, situations and even your own behaviors that try to take your power or your light away from you. This work is something that can change your entire life - and flip it upside down at the same time. Take your time and know that not everything has to be implemented immediately - take it one step at a time. One shift at a time.

We'll begin this chapter discussing more about energy. This is where the real work comes in as far as creating abundance, because abundance IS an energy. It's not a tangible thing. When we understand how to work with energy and the Laws of the Universe, life becomes a lot more effortless and simple.

> *"Our deepest fear is not that we are inadequate. Our deepest fear is that we are powerful beyond measure. It is our light, not our darkness that most frightens us. We ask ourselves, Who am I to be brilliant, gorgeous, talented, fabulous? Actually, who are you not to be? You are a child of God. Your playing small does not serve the world. There is nothing enlightened about shrinking so that other people won't feel insecure around you. We are all meant to shine, as children do."*   - Marianne Williamson

What instructions are you giving to the Universe?

#SacredWealth

ABUNDANCE PRINCIPLE 13 : UNDERSTAND YOUR TRUE POWER

A massive component of understanding our power is dismantling what we were taught about how the world really works and understanding that it is all about energy.

Energy is what runs our world, contrary to what we were taught. Everything is just energetic. We create our reality through our energy and our vibration. **Our understanding of how energy works is the key to our success!** In the most basic terms, we attract what we are being. What does that mean? Well, what we are being is made up of what we think, speak and do. We are always attracting from our energetic vibration.

We all know a Negative Nancy. Isn't it interesting how she seems to continue to attract crappy circumstances to her? This is because she is committed to focusing on negativity, so she attracts more of it. Meanwhile, Positive Polly down the street notices every rainbow and butterfly and her life seems to just get better and better. When something "bad" happens to Positive Polly, notice how she looks for the good in it, and she seems to be really happy and attract amazing things in her life? Everything is energetic - and the Universe follows energetic instruction.

I'd like to start this conversation with an example, so that you can see that you are already very in tune with energy. Imagine Mary - she starts off every morning turning on the news while she drinks her coffee. She listens to the stories about the violence that happened one city over. She watches the mother cry out for her missing daughter. She feels sorry for the person whose house caught on fire that lost everything. Mary then drives to work.

Joanna starts her day a little bit differently, waking up and making her coffee, but instead of turning on the television, she moves over to her meditation mat and lights a candle on the table in front of her. She sits down with her legs crossed and drapes a beautiful blanket over her lap. Joanna reaches for her journal and sets it beside her, in case she wants to jot down any ideas or thoughts she has while doing her morning practice. She turns a timer on for 20 minutes and spends some time deep breathing, followed by journaling before she starts her work day.

When you read both of those examples, do you feel any different? If so, you are noticing differences in energy. Mary's morning experience has her feeling sadness, pity for others or fear for her own safety or for that of her children. Joanna's experience likely created a feeling of calm, peace and tranquility. Now, both women are creating their days from that energy and are likely to attract more of things that bring those feelings for them in their life. The more time we spend in a certain feeling, the more of it we will attract. This is the Law of Attraction. If Mary is feeling scared about life because she spent her morning watching the news, she's more likely to attract sadness, pity or violence into her life. Joanna is much more likely to attract more peace and tranquility - because that's where she is vibrating energetically.

You Already Have the Tools - They Just Need to Be Tapped Into and Used

You are an energetic being and were born with all of the technology needed to read, feel and see energy. Your energetic tools are the greatest wealth you can have, in my opinion. These tools may be a little rusty and require some practice and re-learning, but you are already aware of energy, even if you think you are not. It's like a software update on your phone - the program is already installed, but it may just need an update. You can create this upgrade through practicing the art of tuning in. Check in - have you experienced any of these?

- Has someone ever just given you a bad vibe and you don't know why?
- Have you ever felt drained when you are in the room with a certain someone?
- Do some people make you feel more energized?
- Have you ever randomly thought about someone and then they called you?
- Have you ever seen someone walking down the street and had a random thought pop in your mind about their well-being, with zero other information provided?

Told you! You already experience feeling energy all the time.

The Universe Will Support Whatever You Request

Once we start to understand energy, we realize that we're always attracting things to us or repelling them, through the Law of Attraction. The Universe is only following your instructions. It is so supportive of you - that it will literally show you how well it listens by carrying out any instruction that you offer. **The only instructions we can offer are what we think, feel, say and do** - in other words, our vibrational point of attraction. Our way of being. This tells you how important giving the right instruction is!

The money stories and root beliefs that we spoke about in the Root Chakra section are a significant portion of our energetic instructions towards the Universe. So, if we want to see a change, we must change our instructions!

The remainder of this book will teach you how to do this. *Sacred Wealth* is focused on wealth and abundance, so we will be gearing this conversation towards money, but I want to start out saying that this conversation applies to every area of life - not just money. You can utilize these same principles in your love life, your career, your confidence, your friendships - literally, anywhere.

Let's Talk Money

Money is completely neutral in itself - it doesn't carry any energy other than what you've applied to it.

One person may love money while another may curse money, blaming it for all of their problems. These are their energetic instructions to money, and money listens to them. Money is just an expression of our physical currency today and falls under the same laws of the Universe as everything else does. So, can you agree that it is in our best interest to remove our negative beliefs about money and apply supportive ones so that we can have the experience with wealth and abundance that we desire?

We must offer instructions that match up with what we desire in life. Money listens to us and mimics our vibration, sending it right back to us in the form of abundance. Not only is the Universe and the energy of Money listening, but your subconscious mind is also listening. Your subconscious mind wants to protect you - it wants you to be safe and it uses your belief system to determine what is safe and what is not. So, if you hold a belief that people "with money" are "bad" in any way, your subconscious mind will do everything in its power to keep you from being one of those people. See a few examples below:

> *You*: "Ugh I never seem to have money in the bank."
> *Universe*: "Got it, no money in the bank. I'll keep showing you that."
>
> *You*: "Those greedy men throw money around like it's nothing.They have too much money for their own good. They don't even know what to spend it on!"
> *Subconscious Self*: "I don't want to be greedy, so I don't want money."
>
> *You*: "I work so hard but I never seem to keep any of my money. I'm sick of living paycheck to paycheck."
> *Universe*: "Got it - never want to keep any of your money and you'd like to continue living paycheck to paycheck. Done."

It's so important that we take a real, honest look at who we are BE-ing in our day to day life so that we can become aware of what vibration we are emanating from most of the time. That will show us how we can create subtle shifts in our ways of being to create what we desire.

Let's dive into where your energy is at regarding money, abundance, prosperity, wealth, financial health, etc, using a scale of 1-10. 1 represents total pessimism and the scale moves forward through to complete abundance, optimism or appreciation at 10.

On a scale of 1 - 10, where do you think your energy (thoughts, words, behaviors) falls on a daily basis in regards to financial success and abundance?

What instructions have you provided to the Universe in the past through your energy and thoughts about money, wealth and abundance?

What instructions are you providing to the Universe now through your energy and thoughts about money, wealth and abundance?

What instructions would you like to direct the Universe to create now? This is where you can focus shifting your vibration as you continue your abundance practice.

We attract what we are being. One huge area I see so many of us suffer in is the belief that we must work hard in order to be successful. When we have that belief, we are radiating that energy out to the Universe in everything we do. So, as the loving Universe does, it's going to model that back to us and we will physically "find" evidence that you indeed, must work hard to create money. Our subconscious always wants to be right.

The problem is when our subconscious belief is harmful, and we are still fighting for it to be true. You can always refer back to the Root Chakra section when old beliefs present themselves that you'd like to shed.

When you are taking action, what thoughts and motivation are behind that action?

If you had to describe how you BE - not how you do things, or what you do - but HOW you are in most situations *regarding abundance, wealth and finances*, what would you say? A few examples are listed below for convenience.

Fearful	Grateful	Resourceful	Paranoid
Hopeful	Loving	Victim Mentality	Happy
Excited	Cruel	Manipulative	Stressed
Enthusiastic	Jealous	Responsible	Anxious
Pessimistic	Abundant	Trusting	Worried

Or, insert any words that pop up for you:

Is that way of operating through life creating what you desire?

Great job with the first look at where your energy is vibrating from right now. Re-framing your mindset around money, wealth and abundance basically means that you have to remove all the conditioning from your life that hasn't served you in this area. This is going to take commitment, persistence, effort, dedication and work, especially when you first begin playing with this! We have to unlearn so much of what we've been told, taught and believed since our childhood. This is some of the most valuable work you could ever do because when you are emanating that which you desire, life will become a lot easier and on top of that, you are also raising the vibration of the planet. This work helps yourself as well as the people around you, even if they aren't aware of it.

Our thoughts are direct instructions to the Universe.

#SacredWealth

ABUNDANCE PRINCIPLE 14 : CHOOSE YOUR THOUGHTS CAREFULLY

It all starts in our thoughts. **What we think about is a direct instruction to the Universe.** First, we think about something. It seems innocent, but then we think that same thought so many times that it turns into something that we talk about. Then we act from it. Our thoughts are not innocent, quiet little subtleties that don't result in anything. They are the seed that we do everything from. We have to start to get to a place where we audit our thoughts and do not allow certain thoughts in our mind. I learned about managing my thoughts significantly in 2014 and now I am so aware of the thoughts that pop in my mind, if something comes in that feels insecure or feels bad to my system, I will literally say "DELETE! I didn't mean it!"

You know the crazy thing about thoughts, though? Most of them are subconscious. It is estimated that we have between 60,000 and 80,000 thoughts per day. Most of them are repetitive and we might not even be aware of them. The best way to get familiar with your thoughts is to get still. If we don't ever spend any time in stillness, there is no way we can know what's really going through our mind during the day because we are too busy to hear them.

Most of us don't have any moments of silence in our days - maybe you drive to work with the radio on, hear other people talking all day at work, listen to a podcast during your workout and then watch tv when you get home. **Spirit talks through silence.** Unlike the ego, it does not scream. It whispers. So we have to get quiet enough to hear it. When you get quiet, you can actually start to notice your thoughts.

Yoga practice is the perfect place to notice this. You're in the studio taking a vinyasa class, "forced" to be quiet and focus on your breath. Has this ever happened in your mind, too?

- Who even decided that Crow needed to be a pose, anyway? Why is it even called crow? No one looks like a crow as they are in this god-awful positioning. I think my wrists might *actually* break, I should come out of the pose. Really though, I wonder if crows are accepted with other birds, it seems like they might be the outcasts of the bird family.

- Could the guy next to me breathe ANY louder? *eye roll*

- Ok, Becky in the front row, I don't need you to show off your perfect split as I have 13 blocks supporting me so I don't rip a hamstring today. *reminds myself that I am perfect as I am*

- What shoes should I wear with that new outfit I bought today? *goes through entire closet of shoes and imagines trying them on with the outfit and walking down the Victoria's Secret catwalk*

So, where do we even start to begin the process of managing our thoughts?

It's almost like an auditing process - we need to see what spiderwebs and cobwebs are in there, so we can clean them out, first. Then after that, we replace them with thoughts that serve us or help us manifest what we desire.

The trick is learning to *observe the thought* - not diving into it, not getting emotionally involved in it, not acting like we are Detective Benson from Law and Order: SVU and have to solve the case... **we just observe and let it pass.**

Here are some ways that I will visualize this:

1) Imagine a chalkboard. Everytime a thought pops up, imagine it written on the chalkboard and then see it being erased.

2) See the blue sky above you. As each thought comes in, imagine it showing up inside a cloud, and then you watch it glide on by, out of your peripheral vision.

3) Imagine a briefcase next to you. Visualize writing out the thought on an index card and then opening up your briefcase and putting the index card inside. Close it up.

4) Acknowledge the thought and say to yourself, "interesting." and go back to what you were doing.

When thoughts arise, they are just asking to be audited.

Just because a thought pops up does not mean that it is true. "Hi! I am popping up in your brain. Is this something that I want to keep thinking about? Is this worth my time? Is this worth my energy?" We can retrain ourselves over time to learn to just observe our thought patterns.

How to Rewire Our Thought Patterns:

Many of us are so addicted to stimulation and constantly doing something, that the idea of sitting still for a moment is somewhat terrifying. We let our mind trick us into thinking it's "boring" or we "don't have time"- but really, we are just not used to being in stillness! We also may just be nervous about what is going to come up if we are actually still for 5 seconds. The whole purpose of this initially is just to see what thoughts come up so that you can become aware. If we are repeating so many of the same thoughts each day, imagine how much energy and time we could get back if we transformed those into useful thoughts that could help us manifest the abundant life we desire.

To observe our thoughts, we have to create a practice of stillness. There are many ways to create stillness - but these are some of the tools that have supported me most. I've ordered these from the "least still" to "most still" so that if you are afraid of meditating or have developed a story that "meditating is the worst," you can't escape this principle and have something to try!

1) **Do a yoga class - either in the studio, or a virtual class.**

   Notice the thoughts that come up without any judgment. Purely observing.

2) **Driving in the car in silence - no music, no conversations, no podcasts, no radio**

   This is an amazing way to notice your thoughts and is something you probably do often, anyways, so you don't need to add it to your "to do list." I told you, I'm not giving you any opportunities to skip this - managing your thoughts is literally the most important thing on the planet that you could do. It will 100% change your life.

   Driving with no distractions, at minimum, will clearly show you how you react to other drivers on the road and how you let it affect your own energy. For some reason, we all seem to have a lot of commentary about other people's driving, and this is one of those uses of energy that is purely useless and wastes our energy.

   > Driving Sanity Tip: I tell myself that everyone is either on the way to the hospital for the birth of their first baby, or, that they are about to pee their pants and need a restroom immediately. Both of these make me a much more compassionate driver! Try them on next time you drive.

3) **Taking a walk in silence by yourself - no music, no phone use, no podcasts**

   We store a lot in our bodies, so whenever we move, it's likely that we will have thoughts or emotions come up in some form or fashion. Allow them to move and practice the "observe and release" tactic we talked about above.

4) **Silent Observation of life, doing nothing, with your eyes open for at least 10 minutes.**

   Yes, you heard me right. Do nothing. Just sit there and observe life.

5) Meditation

Meditation is the most supportive way to train ourselves to really be in a position to observe our thoughts. The trick for me has been to make meditation casual - not to make it mean too much, or have the expectation of experiencing pure bliss. It's purpose is just to notice what comes up. After you practice for a while, you'll notice that some days you have a lot of thoughts and other days you can get into that "no space" zone of meditation, that everyone raves about, very easily.

What supports me while I'm in meditation is to bring a notepad and pen with me, and when a thought pops up that does feel important (be very discerning here), I'll jot it down and then get back into the meditation. I only do this now because sometimes I'll get really profound ideas that I will forget because I'm in that "no space" zone. However, don't let your mind trick you here and be writing something down like "Ask hubby if he wants to watch Boy Meets World on Netflix tonight."

> **Remember: Spirit talks through silence.**

How do you feel initially about creating a stillness practice? Have you done this before, or do you currently have a practice of doing this daily? If so, what has your experience been like?

Which of these tools are you going to commit to practicing for at least a few minutes each day this week? I'd recommend starting with at least 10 minutes. The first few minutes may be squirmy, so allowing yourself a little more time will let you get into some juicy thoughts.

Let's do a mini-practice right now.

Please take 5 minutes or so to sit down in a comfortable position, close your eyes and just notice your breathing. Take a few deep breaths and relax. How was the experience?

What thoughts popped up?

How often do you find yourself thinking about these things?

How many times would you guess that you think about them per day?

You will start to notice the quality of your thoughts as you practice stillness more often and from the space of awareness, be able to determine if they are worthy of being in your precious brain or not, impacting your day and your quality of life.

Ask yourself these questions to continue auditing your thoughts:

- Are these thoughts making my life better?
- Are my thoughts mostly about myself or others?
- What is the general essence/vibe of my thoughts?
- What mood do my thoughts put me in?
- How old are these thoughts?

Another way to tune into your thoughts is to notice what you think when you are really happy or really upset. This can sometimes be where the highly repetitive (and taught) thought patterns come into play.

When things wouldn't go my way, I used to repeat in my mind "things just never can be easy, can they?" Talk about a gross thought....that is only manifesting more difficulty and challenge in my life. I will still notice this come up every blue moon because it is so ingrained in me. Because I know better now, when it does come up, I tell myself "DELETE, DELETE, DELETE that from my thought patterns. I am grateful and know that everything is happening on purpose."

What do you typically think when you are happy, confident and loving life?

What do you think when things don't work out? Are there any particular phrases that come to mind?

If you took a snapshot of yourself and could see all the thoughts you have around money, what are the top 5?

This process is a long one - don't expect perfect performance after a month of doing this. This is a lifelong process. I'm 10+ years into this work and I still catch stuff all the time. It's not about being perfect - it's about being aware and intentional.

You were made perfectly, exactly as you are. Don't believe any other lies your doubt may tell you.

#SacredWealth

ABUNDANCE PRINCIPLE 15: FALL IN LOVE WITH YOURSELF

Loving who you are can sometimes seem taboo.... I'm sure you've heard people say things like "she's so full of herself" or "who does he think he is?!" There's a difference between loving yourself and being arrogant. It's time that we make loving ourselves NORMAL and not associated with ego or lack of humility. Loving yourself doesn't mean that you think you are better than everyone on the planet - it just means that you appreciate, respect and honor yourself for the beautiful human that you are. We are basically taught that it's normal to self-deprecate, speak poorly about ourselves and that it's toxic to actually think we are awesome humans.

This activity will help you remember who you are and how wonderful you really are, despite what your meaner thoughts may tell you on some days. Below are some descriptive words for ideas to support you in these prompts:

Powerful	Smart	Outgoing
Intuitive	Adventurous	Thoughtful
Wise	Fun	Insightful
Friendly	Intelligent	Talented
Ambitious	Vibrant	Patient
Sincere	Enthusiastic	Kind
Sophisticated	Big-Hearted	Joyful
Genuine	Playful	Motivated
Outspoken	Genuine	Passionate
Bold	Down to Earth	Pleasant
Considerate	Trustworthy	Gentle
Generous	Attentive	Easy-going
Modest	Curious	Calm
Inspiring	Devoted	Brilliant
Eloquent	Peaceful	Funny
Thoughtful	Energetic	Courageous
Sweet	Fierce	Confident

What are 10 qualities about yourself you really love?

What are 5 things people say about you often to compliment you?

What are 5 challenges you've overcome?

What are 5 qualities that make you an excellent friend, partner, parent, son/daughter, etc?

What are your top 5 favorite words listed from all of the prompts above? Write them below.

I like to create "I AM" boards to remind me of who I am and where I'm going. Our thoughts about ourselves (and everything) inform the Universe about what to deliver to us, so I always want to make sure that my thoughts are aligned with what I want to create!

Example: At the time of writing this, I have big dreams of being a majorly impactful author who creates work that surpasses my time. I haven't written any books before and have a whole slew of limiting beliefs about this happening. However, I know what I want and I'm not going to allow those small thoughts to hold me back! So, I made an entire "I Am" board about who I'll be as an author in a few years. A few examples of what I included:

- I am an impactful author.
- I create work that surpasses my lifetime.
- I am in high demand for my writing abilities.
- I have been recognized globally for my writing.
- I love reading letters from my readers about how my writing has supported them.

In the past, some of my biggest work was believing that I could create a life different than what I saw everyone living around me, so my "I Am" statements were a little bit different:

- I am worthy of creating a life I'm obsessed with.
- I am influencing others to follow their hearts and live life according to their Soul.
- I am a powerful human who creates what I desire with ease.
- I am confident in my abilities and skills.
- I am completely in love with who I am and how I live my life.

Now, it's your turn to create some "I AM" statements to remind you of how amazing you are and help support your thoughts moving in the direction of the life you truly desire:

Mirror Work

Mirror work is a highly valuable tool to help support you in loving yourself more deeply. Mirrors are an amazing way for us to see how we really feel about ourselves. The amount of healing that we can do with a simple mirror is enormous : healing our insecurities about our bodies, connecting with our inner child, doing past life soul exploration, learning to truly see yourself, loving yourself more - the list is endless.

What is your relationship to mirrors? Do you avoid them? Do you look at your reflection in any possible moment? Somewhere in between?

When you look in the mirror, what do you see?

What judgments do you make when you see yourself in the mirror? These could be "negative" or "positive" judgments.

What are you looking for when you look in the mirror?

These questions mostly look at our physical nature. If you found a lot of insecurity within these questions, I would suggest that you take on a practice of looking at yourself in the mirror every day for a few minutes, completely naked. This is going to allow you to hear the thoughts that come up for you most often and you can start to shift the conversation in your mind to focusing on how beautiful, handsome, attractive and lovely you are. Louise Hay talks about "ejecting a CD from your forehead with the old thoughts" so that you can create a whole new set of thoughts. Let's go a little bit deeper now.

When you look in the mirror, who do you see?

What non-physical qualities would you use to describe the person you see in the mirror?

Have you ever looked yourself in the eye? Have you locked eyes with yourself in the mirror?

Now we are getting into our Soul work ; our Spiritual work. Many of you have likely heard the phrase "we are just souls living in skinsuits." Who we are inside has nothing to do with what we look like. Take some time to truly connect with your Soul! One way that you can do this is through locking eyes with yourself in the mirror for at least 4 minutes. The first minute you will probably be squirmy and awkward, but when you give yourself some time, you'll be able to access such deeper levels of yourself. The first time I spent 10 minutes doing this, I started to see visions of my past lives and connected with myself in a way that I had never done before.

There are so many routes we could go with mirror work. If this calls to you, play with it! It's an extremely powerful tool to help raise your self-esteem and really see yourself for the powerful human that you are. There is a lot of information online about mirror work and additionally, Lousie Hay has a book called "Mirror Work" if you'd like to work specifically on loving yourself more. If you would like any support with more of the Soul healing, I can support you with that with my energy healing sessions and Akashic Record Readings.

No one can take your power without your permission.

#SacredWealth

ABUNDANCE PRINCIPLE 16: STOP THE ENERGY LEAKS

Imagine your connection to your energy like a hose filled with water. If there is a leak in your hose, you're losing valuable and precious water! This same thing can happen in our energetic container. The next few principles are going to focus on how we can patch up the leaks we have in our energetic center, so that we can maximize our energy.

The first major area of leakage that we will discuss is in relation to other people. Often we are going throughout our days, sprinkling our power here and there, giving it to anyone who asks for a little taste. There are so many ways that we allow others to take our power - but what's important to really sit in is that we are the ones who are ultimately allowing it. This can range from something small that happens once, to a pattern of giving our power away, to a serious violation of our being that shakes us to our core. When something happens to us, it's not our fault; however, it is our responsibility to choose how we react to it and view it. This is not an easy practice - it is much easier to blame others and choose to be in a victim mentality. However, that kind of thinking keeps us stagnant and usually highly unhappy.

Let's take a look at some of the most common ways that we are giving our power away to others:

Energy Drain: People Pleasing

People pleasing is ultimately putting everyone else before yourself. It's the desire to make someone else happy, but it usually comes at your own expense. This can often look like saying "yes" to everything, feeling afraid to let someone down, helping others with everything - but then realizing you didn't take care of your own needs. At its deepest, people pleasing is really a reflection of lack of self worth or an unhealthy need for approval and acceptance from others. The hard part with people pleasing is that it usually results in people being taken advantage of, resulting in anger and resentments.

Do you feel like you have any people pleasing tendencies?

121

In what ways are you afraid to say "no" to someone or afraid that standing your ground could result in their disapproval of you or feeling upset with you?

Are there any individuals in your life that you feel take advantage of you or are manipulating you?

Here's the thing. We get to remember that we are the ones in charge of our power. We are always teaching others how to be with us - so if someone is taking advantage of you, it's because you're letting them. (Harsh, I know. Virtual hugs.) We get to create strong boundaries, practice saying "No", and create a habit of choosing our own priorities over others to change these behaviors and patterns in others. I give you permission to make yourself your top priority. This doesn't mean that you abandon those you care about, it just means that you come first.

Think about the people pleasing tendencies and behaviors that came up here for you, as well as the people you feel are taking advantage of you. What boundaries could you create to help implement a new experience with them?

Energy Drain: Spending Time with Energy Vampires

Have you heard this term before? Energy vampires are those people that just feel like they suck out all of your positive energy. The person you dread talking to or that individual who you just feel extremely tired after spending time with. You know who I'm talking about. If you go "UGHH" when someone calls, chances are they are an energy drain on you.

Energy vampires are typically people who are negative or complain a lot - and you notice that they may feel more energized after spending time with you, but you feel drained and empty. This can be a subconscious way for the "energy vampire" to feel better - and if you do not create strong boundaries with them, or eliminate them completely from your life, it will be completely at your expense.

It's really easy to say "Wow, Maria is just so toxic" - but we are the ones allowing the toxic behavior. We are the ones who continue to say "yes, let's go to dinner" when we know that we will wish we didn't when we come home. We are the ones who don't say "let's change the subject" or "do you really want to keep putting your focus on this? It's been years!" when Maria talks about her ex-boyfriend from 12 years ago and repeats the same conversation you've heard 16 times before. We must create boundaries in our relationships with others so that they leave us feeling good!

We must take responsibility to protect our inner power at all costs. We must start paying attention to how we feel around certain people or in certain environments to really understand when we've given someone our power unintentionally.

The first step to really honoring our power and self-worth is identifying the people and activities that "steal our power" most often, so we can eliminate those from our life or learn to create boundaries so that they are healthy spaces for us to be in and around.

Who are the people who leave you feeling drained? Is there a particular behavior that this person does that drains you, or a particular way of being?

123

What activities or tasks leave you feeling drained? Would a different perspective help you to enjoy this activity more? Is this something you want to continue doing or that you could eliminate from your life?

Do you feel like anyone in your life has power over you? (Boss, significant other, friends, parents, family members, neighbors, long lost cousins etc).

What boundaries could you implement to take back some of the power you feel others have over you?

Creating boundaries can be difficult - but enforcing them is where we really create lasting change. People will often push up against your boundaries and question them, or even test them, especially if you haven't enforced them before. Eventually, the people meant to stay in your life will respect you for having boundaries, and it will give them permission to create boundaries in their lives as well.

Examples of some of my personal boundaries:
- My time is SACRED. I guard my time and only say yes to things that truly light me up.
- My dreams are precious and I only share them with people who will respect them and be excited about them. I can't be available for Petty Polly's negativity about my wild vision, especially when I'm still not solid on a certain idea and may be more impressionable to doubt or negativity. My vision is too precious to be shared with just anyone.

- I only ask people for advice who I respect and genuinely want their opinion!
- I change the topic if someone brings unwelcome fear, judgment or hate into a conversation. I'm unwilling to go there.
- My energy and space is special. I don't spend time with anyone unless it feels uplifting to me and an equal exchange of energy - this goes for lunch dates, phone calls, e-mails, etc.
- I only tolerate respect and compassion in my friendships.

List the top 3 areas in your life that feel draining right now to you:

What boundaries could you create in these areas that would create a different experience?

How can you call some of your power back in these areas? This could be a change of perception, implementing a new way of doing something, etc.

What would happen if you actually shined at your brightest setting?

#SacredWealth

ABUNDANCE PRINCIPLE 17: LET YOUR LIGHT SHINE BRIGHT

Another major area that we create energy leaks is with our own diminishing habits, behaviors and thoughts. I could write an entire book on the ways that we do this, so we'll just cover the most common ways this can show up here.

How Do You Talk About Yourself?

Often, we learn how to talk about ourselves from what others say to us, what we hear them saying about themselves and what they say about others. We subconsciously pick up this language over time and then direct it at ourselves. Many times, what we are saying to ourselves is just a copy of what we've heard.

When I was a teenager, I remember I was babysitting a young girl who said "I am so fat! I need to work out!" She was about 4 or 5 years old at the time. She likely heard her mother and sisters say that, on top of hearing about losing weight and dieting from television, commercials, other family members, etc. This is just an example of how most of the time, what we think about ourselves is completely untrue but comes from someone close to us. When we repeat that thought enough, we will believe it and start to attract evidence that it is true.

I was a complete beanpole as a teenager. I was 5'11 and weighed about 130 pounds. I don't think I had an ounce of fat on my body. However, I look back at photos and can remember thinking that I was overweight - I would do hours of cardio and eat 1,200 calories a day or less to make sure that I didn't gain weight. This was modeled behavior. I told myself that I was fat so many times, that I attracted more opportunities to view myself in that light rather than seeing myself as natural. I would zone in on the centimeter of skin hanging over my jeans, rather than focus on the lean, tall beautiful girl in the photo. Do you relate to this at all?

We all have areas that we are insecure in, before we create confidence and truly see ourselves as the powerhouses that we are. Some of us are more insecure in what we physically look like. Some of us have more insecurity in our intelligence. Others feel a lack of confidence in their self-expression. Most humans have areas in which we lack confidence, but focusing our thoughts there will only create unnecessary suffering. We get to use our thoughts to build ourselves up, so that we can shine bright (like we are meant to)!

This behavior gets to stop with us. It doesn't get to be passed along any further. Create a pact with yourself that you will only speak kindness to yourself and will not allow others to speak poorly about themselves around you.

What are the things you say about yourself most often that are negative or mean?
List them all here (and then write "LIE" next to it).

What areas of yourself do you attack most?

Did someone in your life do this as well that you could be modeling this behavior from?

When I catch myself saying something mean to myself, these questions always put me in my place quickly:

- Would I ever say this to anyone else? To my best friend or to a child?
- What would I do if someone else said this to me? How would I react? Would I allow it?
- What would I do if I heard my best friend saying this about herself?

It's really easy for us to be incredibly hard on ourselves and say things that we'd never in a million years say to someone else, or even think about allowing someone else to say to us.

When you catch yourself in this pattern of self-deprecation, I want you to stop yourself and say:

Interesting, where did that come from?

Being cruel to yourself isn't going to make anything better, ever. Stop it! Instead, choose to see the hidden benefits in the cruel comment. For example, I've always been an introvert so since the time I was a small child, I've heard others say "oh, she is just shy" so many times that I started to take that identity on myself and repeat it to others. Yes, I may act shy sometimes, but that comes with a lot of incredible qualities, like "I am so observant", "I am a great listener", "When I choose to share, it is highly valuable", "I am selective with who I allow in my space." Allow yourself to see the gold and focus on that, instead.

Toning Ourselves Down to Fit In

Unfortunately, many people are highly uncomfortable with themselves and therefore don't approve of others being completely comfortable and in love with themselves! How many times have you heard someone say "who does he think he is?" Loving yourself doesn't mean that you are arrogant. It just means that you love and accept yourself. What's the better alternative? Is it better to be completely self-loathing? (NO).

In order to accommodate others, sometimes we will tone ourselves down. We ultimately do this to avoid making others uncomfortable, or to protect ourselves from rejection, ridicule, or the pain of feeling left out or alone. Ambitious individuals especially tend to dim their light as to not outshine their partners, parents, siblings, friends, etc. Accomplishments and wins are downplayed, or we can even limit how much effort or how hard we try so that we don't outshine others. The subconscious motive is that we love others so much that we don't want to make them feel uncomfortable or lesser than, but that comes at our expense. It's also actually not loving at all, because we are playing into someone else's fear that could be very healing for them if faced with love.

There are many ways we can tone ourselves down - sometimes this could look like:

- Downplaying an experience we've had or an accomplishment so that we don't make someone else feel inferior
- Acting in a certain way, so that we are approved or accepted
- Changing your expression so that you don't feel like you're being "too much"
- Minimizing your excitement about something
- Substance abuse (numbing yourself)
- Not fully expressing yourself in fear of someone's reaction
- Holding back your talents
- Agreeing in a conversation just to avoid having to share your true feelings

You get to be yourself - you were made as a custom order and are meant to be in full expression of that! When we aren't in full expression of ourselves, we feel limited. That limitation makes us feel depressed, sad, resentful and lethargic. We don't know it, but we are grieving who we could be and are choosing not to be, day after day.

> Think about it this way : what if Beyonce had never left Destiny's Child or Justin Timberlake had never left N'Sync in fear of outshining their bandmates? What if Drake never left Degrassi in fear of failure or trying something new?
>
> **The entire music industry would be different.**

What behaviors are you engaging in that dim your light?

What would change if you were in full self-expression?

How would your life shift if you were fully expressing yourself?

What relationships would be affected most and what would change within them?

"It is not your responsibility to babysit people's insecurities. You are not obligated to slow down your bloom so they can meet you at a level they are comfortable with. Your growth is too important to dim the light within you for someone still trying to find their own."

- Billy Chapata

Where are you placing a limit on the amount of joy you could experience?

#SacredWealth

ABUNDANCE PRINCIPLE 18: SPOT YOUR SELF SABOTAGE

There is an absolutely amazing book that I recommend to many of my clients called "The Big Leap" by Gay Hendricks. I'm going to be borrowing some of his language for today's work, because I don't think anyone explains resistance quite like he does. Please go get the book - it's one you'll read over and over in different times of your life.

We all face resistance when we are growing. Sometimes when that resistance shows up, we respond with self-sabotage.

Think about a few of these situations... you'll likely recognize them :

- "I have so much stuff to do!" .... Takes a nap and avoids it all or starts a new Netflix series
- "Everything has been so great with my partner lately!"..... Starts a fight
- "This book is going to be so fun to write!" ....stares at wall for 6 hours with no ideas
- "I'm going to slay this project".... Reorganizes closet for 2 days

Resistance is smart - it's a mechanism of our ego. Our ego senses danger and tries to protect us. Losing weight or taking on a new project may not feel dangerous to you, but to your ego, it is something NEW and it's very unsure about it. "Is this safe? Is it ok for her to feel that sexy? What will happen? Is it ok to triple the income this year? What will happen?"

The ego gets a bad rap, but it's truly just trying to protect us. It often tries to keep us safe through resistance and sabotage. This resistance is smart. It knows what will work - and when a form of resistance doesn't work anymore, it will update!

When I started my coaching business in 2016, I would get so nervous before sales calls and started to develop this pattern of getting really sleepy before I'd have a sales call. I figured out the pattern and would drink coffee an hour before my call to give me some energy. The resistance saw that I was catching on, and transformed. Then I'd get debilitating migraines or back pain and would have to cancel my call. That lasted until one day I said "Interesting. This is only happening when I'm about to do something scary, so this is just another pattern of my ego." I went on the call, with a migraine, and continued to do so. What do you know, the pattern stopped.

Then it turned into a rampant need to clean in that exact moment, work on another project, scroll Instagram for 6 years, etc. We just have to be able to recognize the resistance and the form of sabotage it takes in order to stop it. The question that helps me most to determine what's really going on is:

> "Am I avoiding something right now?"

Can you tell when your body is in resistance? What does that feel like?

How does resistance show up for you most often? What are the excuses you make the most as to why you didn't complete something? Sometimes, our excuses can be an easy way to spot resistance.

The author of The Big Leap, Gay Hendricks, describes us as all having "upper limit problems." We can only hold a certain amount of joy, before it stretches us too far and we just can't hold it, so we self-sabotage our joy, plummeting us into a lower vibration. This is a pattern of humans - we all do it. Our job is to stretch how much joy we can hold on a daily basis and when we do feel resistance, be willing to sit with it instead of just going with it automatically.

Get in the practice of asking yourself questions like:

- Why am I resisting this?
- What emotion is really coming up right now that I'm trying to avoid feeling?
- What am I afraid of?
- What's my priority right now?

These questions all help you tune into yourself and out of the fear vibration that resistance is often based in. We really get to become clear with the big priority...

> Am I willing to experience more and more joy on a daily basis?
> Am I willing to be more committed to joy than to fear?

Are you willing to feel more joy on a daily basis?

In what area of your life are you upper limiting yourself right now? Where are you placing caps on your happiness?

If you catch yourself acting in self-sabotage, what is something that can bring you back to that commitment to joy? How will you coach yourself in those moments?

Is the energy around you an asset or liability?

#SacredWealth

ABUNDANCE PRINCIPLE 19: CREATE A POWERFUL ENVIRONMENT

Your environment will make or break your abundance and success, because it has such an impact on your state of mind. Our environments, over time, have a huge impact on our quality of life and how we utilize our time and energy. Think about it - if you live with someone who is positive, it's much easier for you to be in a happy, optimistic vibration. If you live with someone who complains about everything, it can feel more challenging to be positive and will be easier for you to go down the negative rabbit hole with your Negative Nancy roommate. We are always intaking the energy around us - so it's important to be surrounded by positivity, love and excitement rather than negativity and pessimism.

Have you heard of Dr. Emoto and his experiments with water? Dr. Emoto believed that energy and vibrations could change the physical structure of water. Based on different environments created through words, pictures or music, he would examine the physical properties of water and how they reacted. Water that was exposed to positive energy, speech and thoughts would result in beautiful snowflake-like crystals in the water structure while the water that was exposed to more negative energy and hateful words would appear blotchy and malformed through his microscopic photography. Just like the water in Dr. Emoto's experiments, our environments physically impact our field of energy.

Let's take a quick inventory of the environment you're surrounding yourself in now. Write down whatever words come to mind first - don't overthink this. Just describe each as the words come to you.

Work Environment:

Home Environment:

The Television / Music / Podcasts/ Media You Watch + Listen To:

Friendship - Support Level:

Romantic Relationships:

What You Eat + Drink:

Where You Live (Home, City, State, Country):

Creating shifts in our environments can be very simple - you don't need to uproot your whole life tomorrow. We can easily add small changes that make a big difference!

Here are a few ideas that I implemented when I started realizing that I wanted to upgrade my environment in all areas of my life:

- Shifting the television I watched to inspiring, educational or happy content. I really enjoy scary movies, but I stopped watching them for the most part because I realized they were giving me nightmares and that it's actually not normal to pop your head out of the shower 16 times in fear that someone is in the house.

- Starting to listen to podcasts that supported my dreams so that I was choosing to listen to people who believed what I desired was possible, instead of people who shared their fears and doubts with me. The positivity outweighed the negativity that I didn't know how to protect myself from at the time, which made a big difference!

- Adding plants into the spaces I hung out in most to raise the vibration!

- Decluttering my life to clear space.

- Creating boundaries in my relationships with others and with self.

- Bringing my salt lamp and several crystals to my cubicle at work to raise the vibration in my workspace.

- Buying an alkaline filter so the water I was drinking wasn't filled with chemicals.

- Ending friendships and relationships that felt toxic.

- Incorporating more color into my wardrobe, home and meals.

- Eating healthier foods that supported my nourishment - not my cravings.

- Diffusing essential oils to elevate my mood.

- Buying flowers when I went to the grocery store as a treat for myself.

- Opening up the blinds, always.

Go back to the inventory above and **rate each area from 1 - 10**, 1 being completely unsupportive, toxic or unhealthy and 10 being supportive, healthy and inspiring.

Write down your lowest three scoring areas here:

What are some simple shifts you can create in these areas?

Area 1:

Area 2:

Area 3:

Start creating shifts in these areas today! Our environment makes a gigantic difference in how we feel on a daily basis. Once you've incorporated those changes, I challenge you to create small shifts in any area that's not a 10!

The other element that we want to look at in our environments is how clean or cluttered they are! Clutter literally makes me crazy. Scientifically, we can prove that clutter increases anxiety and feelings of overwhelm - and when we declutter, we start to feel more calm. How do you feel after you organize a gnarly closet? Pretty on top of the world right?! I always have more energy after cleaning - it makes me feel productive and motivated.

Physical clutter translates to clutter of the mind. When our spaces are cluttered, our minds will feel cluttered. Please bring your attention to your physical locations you spend the most time in: your home, your place of work and your car. I want you to really think about each item in these places and ask yourself the following questions:

- Do I use everything that I have?
- Why am I keeping the items I don't use?
- Do the items I have bring me joy?
- Am I keeping any items because I feel guilty giving them away or selling them, even though I know deep down that I really don't want them? (many of us do this with gifts!)

I have a few rules for myself, because I feel so impacted by clutter:

- I only keep items that I love. Think about the Marie Kondo rule... Does it bring me joy? If not, it goes.
- I only purchase items that I absolutely love. It is way too easy to buy stuff at Target every shopping trip and then there I am again, 8 months later, trying to sell it at Plato's Closet (and most likely being rejected).
- If I receive a gift that I don't like, I will donate it, or if I'm comfortable enough with the person, I will let them know that I appreciate it but I am being really picky with what enters my home and that I want them to receive their money back, or find the receipt so I can exchange it. This might make you cringe... that's why I said I only do this with people I'm extremely comfortable with and won't take it personally! The people close to me all know that I am so picky with what I have at home.

Remember, everything is energy! So every item you own is contributing to the energy of your home. If you really hate that 1976 ceramic figurine that Great Aunt Dora gave you, consider that it's taking up valuable space where more magic could enter.

Commit to going through at least one area of your home this week and clearing out an area! Even just one drawer at a time is a win. If you're like me, and you operate very all -or-nothing, this can be a great weekend project.

Where is the top priority for you to clean out and spend some time decluttering?

Because this book is all about abundance and money, let's take some time to clean your wallet / purse out as well as wherever you keep your financial documents. If you don't use a purse or wallet, just apply this to wherever you keep your money.

I want you to act from now on as if you have purchased a $100,000 wallet. You are going to keep it pristine at all times. You'll treat it like Gold.

<u>Repeat after me:</u> "I will not throw free mints from the bank into my purse. I will not put balled up gum in a wrapper into my purse. I will not ball up receipts and throw them into my purse."

This is a sacred space and you will treat it as such! Your purse and wallet will feel rich, divine and luxurious (no matter what they actually cost). This will feel like an area that is cultivating high frequencies and positive energies with abundance. Pro tip: Always keep cash in your wallet! This will help you to attract more cash as you are used to seeing it in your wallet. Stick a hundred dollar bill in there and just leave it, don't spend it! If this is challenging for you - go re-read the part of the Root Chakra section where we talked about self-sabotaging patterns! So, go ahead and clear it out! A few questions to help you in your decluttering process:

What do you actually need in your purse or wallet? Do you actually need 3 bottles of hand sanitizer, or will 1 do? Are 13 lip glosses really required? Is your YMCA card from 2004 ready to be thrown away yet?

What items feel abundant and high vibrational that you'd like to have in your purse or wallet? I love to keep an abundance stone, like citrine or pyrite, in my purse as well as a golden hundred dollar bill I purchased in Sedona years ago.

Does it make you feel excited to keep change in your wallet? Receipts?

Which do you prefer - cash all facing the same way, flattened and in one place, or cash crumpled up in multiple places?

Remember, money is energy and is a relationship. If your roommate kept the house a complete disaster zone, how would that make you feel? How do you think money feels when your environments you keep it in are gross and dirty, surrounded by balled up receipts from the gas station?

Where is your vibrational point of attraction right now?

#SacredWealth

ABUNDANCE PRINCIPLE 20: CLEAN UP YOUR VIBRATION

The last area we will discuss in regards to the Solar Plexus is our vibrational point. We learned what energy was and how it operates earlier in this section - our vibration is just the "set point" of where our energy is at. This is the place we manifest from! Our Solar Plexus is our place of power, so we want to understand how we can cultivate a powerful point of vibration so we can manifest what we desire from that space.

Our vibration can change from moment to moment, but typically we have an average range that we move from, or a range that we stay in the majority of the time. For example, Negative Nancy stays in pessimism most of the time. She's not vibrating very high, because she's always looking for the problem in everything. She's literally looking for things to be upset about (even if she isn't conscious of this). Positive Penelope, on the other hand, looks for the lesson in everything. She makes everything a learning opportunity and shows gratitude for the challenges in her life, because she knows that they are just a blessing in disguise!

As we briefly discussed before, when we are in a negative vibration, we are only going to attract more negativity because that is the energetic instruction we are giving to the Universe. When we are on the lookout for miracles, we're going to attract blessings and an abundance of appreciation coming to us.

Where do you think your point of vibration is most of the time, in general?

Where do you think your point of vibration is most of the time, relating to your finances?

What we're discussing in this principle is how we can move through challenges and big emotions without allowing them to completely take over our vibration. It is a powerful act to move through our emotions - many have been taught that being emotional is a sign of weakness. The opposite is True. Feeling our emotions takes strength and creates an immense amount of empowerment.

145

We all face challenges and big emotions - and they are literally our guidance system. We don't want to ignore our emotions, because then we are just creating a pattern of suppression. Suppression is when we sweep something under the rug, or stuff it down (" I don't have time or space to deal with this right now" or "I can't face this" vibe). This is incredibly unhealthy for us and I believe it creates dis-ease in our bodies, which can culminate in much more pain than if we would have just dealt with it in the first place!

Feeling our emotions can be really difficult. Facing them head on can range from annoying to agonizing. However, emotions aren't meant to stick around forever - they are just coming up so that we can look at what's causing them and then move through it and release it!

I'm about to get real personal with you to help illustrate how we can move through emotions in a healthy way.

Background: Right now I am single for the first time in almost 9 years at the age of 29. My previous partner and I ended our engagement and I'm living in an Air BnB rental by myself in a small beach town in Florida during the 2020 quarantine season.

There are many emotions rising to the surface - but I want to deal with them now and face them head on so that they don't impact my future relationships in a negative way. So I don't stuff down painful emotions that could later turn into something more toxic in my body. I want to learn the lessons. We have to fully feel the pain attached to these emotions. If we half-ass it, it's just going to stick around longer. There is no avoiding it.

I'm going to try to make this explanation as funny and enjoyable for you as possible - I give you full permission to laugh at me here. I'm laughing as I write it!

Feeling the Emotion Fully

One day, I felt this enormous, soul crushing wave of sadness come out of nowhere. I had been feeling free as a bird, single for the first time as an awakened woman, and was surprised by this feeling. I sat in it and let myself cry, without really knowing what I was crying about. I just felt sadness and let the tears fall, without judging any part of it.

After a few days of these waves of sadness coming in and a couple extremely dramatic, crying sessions in the shower (while obviously playing extremely sad music and singing as loud and dramatically as possible), I felt a pause - an opportunity to evaluate from a clear mind.

Identifying the Emotion

I asked myself "what is this emotion that I'm feeling? Obviously there is sadness. What's underlying the sadness? Why am I sad?"

(Get ready for the dramatic response) - "WELL- I am alone and have no one and my friends aren't there for me in the way I would have expected them to be, and I'll probably be alone for my whole life and I'll probably die alone in this apartment and no one will find me for 700 years and then I'll go into a museum with a title labeled "lonely woman found alone." Just, wow. The drama.

Bringing In Compassion

Then it's time to bring compassion and get even clearer. What's really true?

"I just feel lonely. I'm alone for the first time in a long time, and no one is coming home at the end of the day. I'm almost 30 years old and thought I had my life figured out with a future I could see.... And now all of that is gone. All that's left is uncertainty. I don't want to start over in the romance department, but I know I have to."

Ok - well I could feel that. That's understandable. Then I cried some more. I sat with that for a few days and let myself feel it fully. A few days later, I noticed that I didn't feel as sad about it anymore. I felt neutral. Interesting.

Getting Clearer on What Is True

"Ok, so I do feel lonely. That's understandable. Most people feel lonely in this position and I'm certainly not the only person feeling loneliness right now." Compassion.

More neutrality came - and I remembered who I am - and how I could feel differently.

"Well, I'm kind of choosing to feel lonely because I'm visualizing myself in a museum of humiliation, I'm not calling my friends and telling them that I've been in a 16-day meltdown, and I'm not asking for the support that I know is available if I asked for it."

Choosing How I Want to Feel

"I want to feel supported. I want to feel nurtured. I want to feel loved."

Choosing How To Move Forward

How can I create that for myself?
How can I allow others to support me in feeling this way?

"I can ask my friends to text me often. I can ask my friends to get on a Zoom call. I can do the things that allow me to nurture myself. I can buy myself roses. I can give myself hugs. I can do the things I would want to do with a significant other and enjoy my own company without feeling pity. I can move into appreciation."

Do you see the process I went through? I moved from feeling pure loneliness and pity for myself, to feeling neutral, to feeling supported and finding appreciation.

How I Moved Through the Big Emotions
1. Feeling the emotion fully.
2. Identifying the feeling.
3. Bringing in compassion.
4. Getting clear on what's true.
5. Keep feeling the emotion, until it shifts.
6. Choosing how you want to feel.
7. Choosing how you want to move forward.

This is a process I learned from reading so many of Esther Hicks books, listening to her seminar recordings and watching YouTube videos. I highly recommend her work. I'm going to introduce a concept she teaches called the Emotional Guidance System. This is what I just described in the example of my experience above.

Esther and her guide, Abraham, teach how we can shift to a higher vibration from any emotional state - they use a tool called the Emotional Guidance Ladder to illustrate this. See below.

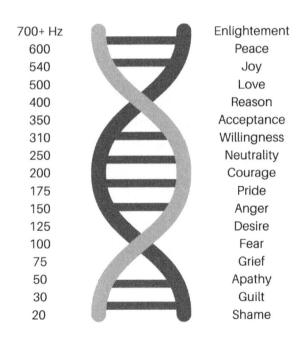

700+ Hz	Enlightenment
600	Peace
540	Joy
500	Love
400	Reason
350	Acceptance
310	Willingness
250	Neutrality
200	Courage
175	Pride
150	Anger
125	Desire
100	Fear
75	Grief
50	Apathy
30	Guilt
20	Shame

You can see how each number on the left corresponds to the vibrational frequency (Hz) of specific emotions. The higher the frequency, the better you feel!

While I was feeling loneliness, I was probably vibrating around the Fear/Grief vibration, which is pretty low on the vibrational scale. However, if I brushed that under the rug instead of feeling it, that would be stuck in my body and I would be attracting from that place. Gross.

Instead, I allowed myself the time and space it took to move up this scale slowly, as I authentically felt these different emotions. I moved through the loneliness to appreciation, which is one of the highest vibrations. Now, if loneliness pops back up, I can remember "ah, I'm so thankful for this feeling of loneliness because it allows me to remember that I actually have so many people in my life that can support me in moving through this. It allows me to appreciate the time I had with my previous partner and how he made me feel highly seen and loved. I'm so appreciative for that kind of experience." I can quickly shift from loneliness to appreciation, without it taking a long time to move through, because I've already done the (shower soundtrack) work of healing the initial wound.

Now - some people linger in emotions and will not ever move through to a higher vibration because some part of them actually wants to stay in the lower vibration. Often this is because we receive attention from feeling this way or because we actually don't want to do the work to shift.

In highschool, I remember there was a girl in my grade who told everyone she had cancer. She was bald and we all thought she was in chemotherapy, even teachers. She had doctor's notes. She missed significant amounts of school. One day, her grandmother came into school and someone said "I hope she feels better! Can I do anything to help?" and the woman was clueless and shocked that her granddaughter had told such an enormous lie for years. This teenager had completely made up having cancer. She likely did this because she received so much attention and somehow she wanted pity from others. Maybe she felt invisible at home and didn't receive the attention she needed, so she acted out and made up an elaborate story to feel seen. This might seem crazy, but it's actually just really sad that this is the only way she could find to feel seen and cared about. She wanted to be vibrating at a low place - to receive more attention- to feel loved.

You probably know someone who is still angry at their ex from 30 years ago. You probably know someone who still has shame about something they did 15 years ago. Holding onto these low vibrational emotions is highly dangerous for our being. We're going to talk about forgiveness and unconditional love in the next section, the Heart Chakra, so if you are one of these people (most of us are holding on to about 1,000 things we can forgive), stay tuned for this.

Now it's time for you to tune into your own emotional being.

How do you normally handle emotions when they come up? Face them? Avoid them?

After reading this, does anything come up that you know you haven't fully allowed yourself to face?

Considering the emotions you've swept under the rug (if you are aware of them), where do you think you lie emotionally on the scale? What are the negative, low-vibrational emotions that you may still be vibrating at towards certain incidents or people? Don't overthink this - name anything that may pop up. There might be alot!

Where do you want to be vibrating at? How do you want to feel?

   The next pages are an opportunity for you to move through two different emotional experiences that you may have swiped under the rug. Don't pretend you don't have any. We all do. This work IS the work of creating more room for abundance in our lives. When we clear out the low vibrational feelings, we can then replace that void with higher vibrations so we are manifesting from that space and attracting miracles!

   Choose whatever your lowest vibration emotion is around - if you'd like to think specifically about your finances - consider shame or guilt in past decisions made or anything else that may come up for you. I recommend moving through the emotions with the most charge that come up. Do this exercise as many times as needed.

<u>**Emotional Experience to Move Through #1:**</u>

Journal about the experience you've wanted to avoid looking at, or the emotions that you haven't wanted to fully feel or experience.

Give yourself space and time to acknowledge what this emotion is and to feel it. If you have space right now, let yourself go there and fully feel it, or create private time later to do so.

What is this emotion telling you? What are you feeling?

How could you see this through the eyes of compassion? If someone else was feeling this, what would you say to them or how would you view them while they're experiencing this emotion? Sometimes, we can be much more compassionate to others than we are to ourselves.

What is the truth about this?

How do you want to feel?

What could support you in feeling this way?

Please imagine me giving you a gigantic, snuggly bear hug. Great work. This takes courage.

Let's look at one more experience that you can shift. Remember, the more low vibrational experiences and emotions we shift, the more room for magic!

Emotional Experience to Move Through #2 :

Journal about the experience you've wanted to avoid looking at, or the emotions that you haven't wanted to fully feel or experience.

Give yourself space and time to acknowledge what this emotion is and to feel it. If you have space right now, let yourself go there and fully feel it, or create private time later to do so.

What is this emotion telling you? What are you feeling?

How could you see this through the eyes of compassion? If someone else was feeling this, what would you say to them or how would you view them while they're experiencing this emotion? Sometimes, we can be much more compassionate to others than we are to ourselves.

What is the truth about this?

How do you want to feel?

What could support you in feeling this way?

You are amazing. Wonderful job, today. I know this was big work - take care of yourself and do whatever you need to do to give yourself a little extra love! PS - I've created a printout of this exercise on my website Book Resources (www.alywilkins.me) if you want to print more of these out and do this exercise again.

ENERGY HEALING: FILLING UP THE SOLAR PLEXUS CHAKRA

When we feel a lack of empowerment, insecure, doubtful or fear of being in our full expression is a perfect time to amplify our solar plexus chakra, our power center.

Visualization:

Lay down and get comfy. Do a quick scan of your body and as you deepen your breathing, begin to relax each part of your body, from the top of your head, down to your toes. Take this process slowly.

Once you are completely relaxed, close your eyes and imagine a great, vibrant yellow orb glowing in the center of your belly. Imagine this orb growing bigger and bigger, expanding from your navel until it grows beyond the size of your whole body. Within this field of vibrant, yellow, now imagine a single yellow rose blooming from your belly button. Imagine that your entire torso is now sprouting yellow roses. See the bright yellow vibration in your mind's eye and notice how you feel!

Physical Tools and Support:

If you feel you've given away your power, do this quick practice:

1) Spread your arms out like you are holding a beach ball.
2) Say "I now call all of my power back to me" while your arms are spread out wide.
3) Bring your arms back into your body, placing your hands over your heart or over your stomach.

A few other tools:
- Start wearing bright colors like yellow or decorating your home with brighter colors.
- Complete a Cord Cutting Ceremony to cut energetic cords with people who may be draining your energy. You can find this description at the Book Resources page at www.AlyWilkins.Me.
- Utilize your Energy Bubble of protection to support you as you spend time with others. You can find this description on my website as well with the Book Resources.
- Create reminders of how powerful you are! Utilize Post-It notes, phone alarms or create your own "I Am" board.
- You can even utilize an Alter Ego! Create one, or use someone that you admire. Tap into their energy field to borrow some confidence. If you need to make an important decision, ask yourself "what would my alter ego do?"
- Read the book "You Are a Badass" by Jen Sincero.

Solar Plexus Chakra Affirmations:

- I am powerful and radiant.
- I am full of joy and bliss.
- I fully own my power.
- I am strong and courageous.
- I give myself permission to be my authentic self.
- I accept myself and love myself unconditionally.
- I am confident in my ability to succeed and accomplish my dreams.

Solar Plexus Crystals:

- Citrine for empowerment, positivity and abundance
- Pyrite for manifesting power, luck and prosperity
- Sunstone for self-esteem
- Labradorite for energy protection
- Carnelian for confidence and vitality

Solar Plexus Chakra Essential Oils:

I like to put these oils on my hands, rub them and then bring them to my face to breathe the oil in. You can also put them directly on the belly, just be cautious with the citrus oils as some can be harsher on the skin.

- Citrus oils like orange or grapefruit for uplifting energy
- Lemon for refreshment and new starts!
- Peppermint for invigorating energy.
- Ginger for activation of the solar plexus.
- DoTerra has an oil called Motivate that I use almost daily!

Heart Chakra

Anāhata

Heart Chakra

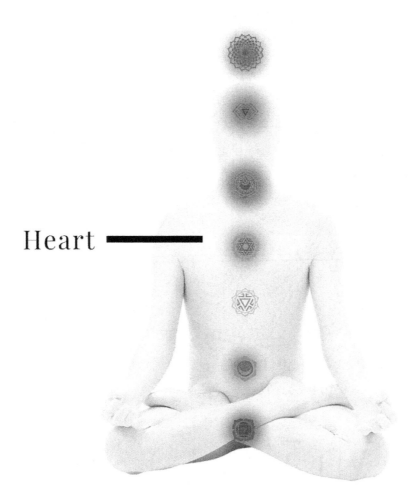

Heart ———

HEART CHAKRA: ANAHATA

Living with an open heart is truly the only way to fully experience life. Most of us are walking through life, armored and guarded like we live in a security system, terrified of letting the full experience of life come in and open ourselves up to potentially getting hurt.

We aren't taught the value of the heart, for the most part. We are taught the value of the mind - and that the heart only comes in play when it comes to love. We are taught to protect our heart from getting hurt. This might save us from the pain of rejection and heartbreak, but are we really living if we aren't open and vulnerable? There's no chance of experiencing the true bliss life has to offer when we are living from a closed off space.

You could have the most money in the world, but if you aren't able to experience joy from a beautiful flower or the deep, intense passion with your guard fully down, you likely are living like a robot - numb, emotionless, unable to fully experience what life has to offer. That's not abundance. That's just going through the motions with a nice boat you can't even fully enjoy. This entire book has been about how we can open up more space in our bodies to feel abundance - and the heart is the biggest area of opportunity for us to let more abundance in.

Every person reading this has most likely been hurt before in life, love and friendships. If you could choose to go back and erase that hurt (but also erase the love, passion and memories), would you? Was the love worth it?(Always). Heartbreak and loss can feel devastating to the Soul. It can feel like it breaks us. But somehow, the heart always heals. The heart always comes back to us - guiding us to another opportunity to feel love.

Love is a blessing that we get to experience - whether it's the love from a significant other that you truly allow yourself to open up to, the love that you feel inside when you pet a cute puppy, the love of life you experience when you achieve something you've always dreamt of, or the unconditional love that you feel when you squeeze your niece's chubby baby legs. We get to choose the extent that we will open it up and allow love in.

This section will be about how you can open more fully and identify where your armor is still up, relating to both life and money (it is all connected, anyway). There are many subtle ways we close ourselves - and we're going to dig into them. Your life is worth experiencing - the highs and the lows. Living in a safe, protected, numb, neutral beige bubble is not living.

The more you open up to life, the more high vibrational experiences and life changing opportunities you open up to. Choosing to live with an open heart allows you to experience more magic than you've likely ever experienced. Total bliss can come from tiny things, when we are open. Imagine seeing a butterfly pass you as you walk down the street and feeling so happy you could cry. Let's bring on more opportunities for those happy tears, shall we?

161

If you want to feel
happier, amp up the
amount of gratitude
you choose to tap into.

#SacredWealth

ABUNDANCE PRINCIPLE 21: CHOOSE TO SEE THE MAGIC

The first place we must rewire in our hearts is how we view our lives. Gratitude seems so basic and simple - and it is. Gratitude is what allows us to see the true beauty in life. Do you know how much magic is sitting right in front of you that you likely aren't even acknowledging? Sometimes we even have the audacity to complain about these things - while others may be wishing and dreaming for that same very thing.

We've all heard the word "gratitude" a million times . We read about it and say internally, "I know, I know" and then proceed to ignore it, thinking it's too simple. Gratitude is the easiest and fastest way to re-train and shift our mind. If you want to grow quickly, all you have to do is amp up the amount of gratitude you feel.

One of the most life-changing moments of my life happened at a stop light. Many of my clients know this as "The Palm Tree Story." It was 2015 and I was so unhappy. I had moved to Orlando about a year earlier with my partner at the time and so many shadows had been presenting themselves: the fear of working in a purposeless career for 50 years, never able to live or experience life in the ways I dreamt about, growing pains in my relationship that made me want to run away everyday, and just the bleak future I saw ahead of me if nothing changed. To say the least, I was agitated, moody and extremely discouraged with what being an adult was supposed to look like.

So, it was a Tuesday morning and I was sitting at this stop light that is the longest stoplight in the history of time. If you missed the small window of green light opportunity, you'd have to sit for 19 minutes to wait for a train, bikers and alligator crossings until the light turned green again. I was already running late and woke up in a bad mood for the 57th day in a row, feeling furious at life that I had 3 more days in the week before the weekend. I looked up, and the car in front of me had stopped at the yellow light, clearly not understanding that the alligators would take 30 minutes to cross before the light would turn green again.

All of the sudden, it was like something picked my chin up and my eyes darted to the gorgeous, tall and thick row of palm trees lining the street behind the stop light. I realized I had never seen them. Never noticed. I passed these palms every single day for half a year and never even saw them. I thought, "how many people wish they could see palm trees everyday? *I'm so used to them that I don't even see them.* **I've been focusing on the wrong things**. "

It was one of the first experiences I had that was a sure sign from Spirit. This moment completely changed my life moving forward. For the first time, I saw the beauty I had been missing right in front of me. I had been choosing to not see this beauty, and instead, to focus on misery. Before, I had been looking for the green or red light only, which would indicate whether I could be happy until the next road block or give me permission to hate the world and my life a little more. I snapped the photo below at this moment, since something in me told me everything after this moment would be different, and it was.

Let's take a quick check in. Honestly - do you focus on the negative or on the positives more often? Consider if you are more negative in certain areas of your life while may be more positive in others (career, family, money, friendships, etc).

It is a survival mechanism for our human brain to focus on the negatives - it is trained to keep us alive and help us survive. We don't need the same survival instincts now that we needed in our caveman days, but many of these mechanisms are still working in the same ways! It's just a matter of starting to re-train ourselves to see the positives. Over time, this shifts and it becomes our natural response. It does take time, but you'd be surprised how quickly this shifts when you are committed.

There's so many ways to make gratitude a super fun process - so let's dive into a few of my favorite methods here!! If you feel tempted to skip this section, it's extra important that you do it!

Bring It Back to the Basics

How often do you really sit in gratitude for the most basic elements of our everyday lives? I always go back and think about how people lived in the 1700's and 1800's - no indoor restrooms, no air conditioning, no electricity or hot water. No refrigerators, dishwashers or stoves. Even today, many people don't have access to running, clean water. Many of us complain about the water being too hot or not hot enough.

Think about our bodies. We've been trained through marketing and the diet industry that there's always something else we can improve in our bodies. I'd love for you to completely trash all of that nonsense. Our bodies, no matter how they look, are working for us without us even knowing it. Have you had to remind your heart to beat before? Have you had to help facilitate your digestion process ever? No. The body does everything for us, on its own. It's a miracle. The next time you start to complain about your body, I want you to think about that!

Consider some of the priceless elements of our bodies that we really don't pay much attention to - our ability to see, hear, smell, taste, touch. The ability of our feet and legs to carry us throughout the day. The gratitude of having hands that help us carry things and hold a million grocery bags at once. Our brain working and functioning properly to support us in making decisions and moving through our days. I often think about how grateful I am for my vision. Could you put a price on that? If so, what would it be? $100 Billion? Wow, how abundant are we?!

What are some of the basic luxuries you experience on a daily basis that you don't think about very often? Name 10+ below.

Basic Gratitude Journaling

I believe the best way to begin your gratitude practice is to bring our attention to gratitude, first thing in the morning, so we are setting the stage for our day from that energy. Here's what my process looks like:

10 New Things I'm Grateful For

Challenge yourself to come up with 10 new things each day! This is super simple. There are millions of things we can be grateful for.

1. I'm so thankful for my ability to see and for my healthy and functioning eyes.
2. I'm so appreciative for my parent's health and vitality!
3. Thank you for blessing me with all four limbs and the ability to walk, climb, swim, etc.
4. I'm so thankful for a door that locks and a roof over my head to help me feel safe.
5. I'm so appreciative for the experiences in my life that have catapulted my growth.
6. I'm so thankful for listening to the call to go to Bali for the first time several years ago.
7. I'm so grateful for my comfortable and fluffy sheets and comforter that keep me warm.
8. I'm so appreciative for having constant access to clean water and hot water.
9. I'm thankful for the privileges I've had as a white American woman.
10. I'm so thankful for the authors who have written books that have changed my life.

Ok, now it's your turn!

10 Things I'm Grateful For

Be Grateful Every Time You Spend Money!

We can bring gratitude into everything we do on a daily basis. One way to magnetize abundance is to bring gratitude every time we spend money!

Often, our response to spending money is something similar to "ugh" or "that's money being taken out of my account" or "there goes my paycheck." That's not very empowering. Money doesn't feel very appreciated. She's like, "You're welcome for the groceries, brat!"

So instead, even if you're spending your last ten cents, try to shift your focus to gratitude. Here's a few examples:

- "I'm so thankful I have the funds to purchase this food! This is going to make some great dinners that will nourish my body and soul."
- "Thank you, cell phone company, for providing me such ease in communicating with the world and having information at my fingertips. What a bargain!"
- "I am so grateful to be able to pay for heat this winter."
- "It makes me feel really great that I can support this local business, even if it costs a little more than supporting a big box retailer. Thank you Universe, for the funds to be able to contribute to a small business and my local economy."
- "Every dollar I spend comes back to me tenfold!"

When you pay your bills or purchase anything, realize that it is a choice. You do not HAVE to pay your electricity bill. You could live without electricity. People did that for a very long time. We have the audacity to be like "UGH, why is air conditioning $100 a month" but would you want to live without it if you live in a place like Florida or Texas? If you had to choose, I'm pretty sure you would choose to pay for the air conditioning. And guess what, if you don't want to pay for the electricity, cut it off! We only want to invest in things that are meaningful to us, so we are truly respecting money!

When you pay your bills the next time, really sit in gratitude that "I am so thankful I can come in and just flip a light switch on instead of having to light 67 candles so I can read my book without obliterating my 20/20 vision. I am happy to pay this bill. Thank you, electric company, for providing me such convenience."

Do you feel that energetic shift? So does the Universe.

How do you usually feel when you spend money?

Do you have any bills that you have a large amount of resentment towards paying? Do you want to keep paying them and using that service? (If not, cancel it!)

How can you shift how you feel when you pay your bills or buy anything?

Other Practices to Amplify Your Gratitude

- Start saying "Thank You" whenever you receive anything - an idea, clarification on something, a physical item - say thank you as much as you possibly can.

- Gratitude Rants
    - Spend a few minutes speaking out loud about what you are grateful for! This energy builds on itself and amps you up!! This is a great activity to do in a solo elevator ride, or waiting in line to pay for groceries, or to do in your drive to work!

- Telling someone that you appreciate them
    - If you want to show more love to those around you, get in touch with someone every day or every week just to let them know you care and appreciate them. This can be a quick text - "thinking about you . love you and appreciate having you in my life! Thanks for being you."

- Bedtime Gratitude practice:
    - Place something on your pillow after you get out of bed in the morning, it could be a crystal, a trinket, a chocolate, literally anything that is large enough that you will notice it before you go to bed. When you see this item on your pillowcase at night, it's your reminder to think about the amazing things that happened that day! Ask yourself "what am I grateful for that happened today?" as you hold your object.

What's one area of your life you know you can bring more gratitude to?

"A spiritual journey is
truly unlearning fear
and remembering love."

GABBY BERNSTEIN

#SacredWealth

ABUNDANCE PRINCIPLE 22: DISSOLVE THE FEAR MINDSET

Fear is a big way that we resist love. Choosing fear comes from our survival mechanism - we need it. It keeps us safe! But the fear that you feel when you're walking down a dark alleyway and hear footsteps behind you is very different from the fears that seem to run rampant in our society today, which mostly revolve more around our ego:

- How will I look if I fail?
- What if I fall flat on my face?
- What if I have to start all over?
- What if it doesn't work out?
- What if I get hurt?

> **Our fears grow the more that we feed them.**

Fear is something we have to get a hold on - otherwise, it can easily take over our entire life. Living life from a place of fear is no way to live. The sad part about this is, most people are doing this very thing. How many people do you know who have a dream that you've heard them talk about, yet they will not act on it from a place of fear?

Where is fear coming up most in your life right now?

Where did this fear come from? We aren't born fearing these kinds of things - we usually are absorbing the fear from someone else, and eventually it feels like it is our own.

What is something you've always wanted to do, but haven't? Why not?

What do you think might happen if you did this? What's the best case? What's the worst case? We don't just live in airy fairy land and ignore real potential consequences of our actions - but we do get to think about how likely they are to happen.

Are the people around you constantly reminding you of everything you have to be afraid of? If so, start finding examples of individuals who stretch themselves and live boldly - and paying less attention to those who spread fear. It is literally a virus that is toxic to your system.

How can you create boundaries so that you don't absorb this fear?

Who are a few people who inspire you that seem to live life with little fear? People who courageously go after what they desire? (and how can you listen to them more often?)

What fears do you have around your financial state?

What is the biggest fear that you have that impacts your everyday life?

How could you view this from a different perspective? What other ways could you see this so it doesn't feel so terrifying?

FEAR = False Evidence Appearing Real. Be careful how much weight you give it in determining your life. Not doing things because of fear leads to a life of regret.

> *"I was thinking... if I cheated on my fears, broke up with my doubts and got engaged to my faith, then I could marry my dreams."*
> - Beyoncé

How we judge others is just a reflection of how we judge ourselves.

#SacredWealth

ABUNDANCE PRINCIPLE 23: REMOVE THE POISON OF JUDGMENT

Judgment of any kind is a low vibration. It repels money, happiness and feeling good.

First of all - let's get clear that we all judge, all day long. We can't survive without making judgments. We have to make judgments in order to make any kind of decision. For example, is this spinach so questionable that I shouldn't eat it? Are my car tires full enough, or could I possibly be in danger if I don't add some air? How long can I wait, because I really don't feel like doing it today. Is this person trustworthy enough for me to confide my deepest secret with them? These are the kinds of judgments that we need to make decisions - this section is referring to the poisonous, critical judgments we do not need.

Many of us grow up hearing judgment about other people in many ways, especially when it comes to money. A few examples of what I heard from people around wealth:

- "People who make millions of dollars are greedy. They did something bad to earn their money. They are probably using others to do all the hard work for them. It's not fair. "
- "I feel so sorry for (insert many kinds of occupations). They work so hard and make such a small salary for the important work that they do. They deserve to make more money. "
- "She bought what?! She is so irresponsible."
- "Who does he think he is, buying that car? What a show off."
- "That person is in the situation they are in because they don't work hard enough. They are lazy."
- "Don't marry a poor guy. He won't be able to take care of you."
- "They spent way too much on that outfit."
- "They should be spending more responsibly."

And the list could go on and on . Guess what - everyone has different priorities and we are not the high and mighty ones who have been selected to cast judgement upon everyone.

Judgment is a low vibration - it doesn't matter what you're talking about or if you're "right" or not. Judging anyone brings down your vibration, and what we know about abundance is that the higher you vibrate, the more abundance you'll experience.

Additionally, we're always providing directions to the Universe, remember? If you are complaining about Lebron James making so much money, all your subconscious hears is "people who make that kind of money are bad people and I don't want to be a bad person, so I'm definitely never going to allow myself to make that kind of money."

Do you want to be in judgment? No one really feels good (on the inside) as they are casting judgments on someone else. The people who judge the most also judge themselves the most. The happiest people I know are also the least judgmental

The happiest people that I know are the least judgmental.

Judgment is a huge energy drain, a complete waste of energy and only lowers your own vibration. Here are a few ways we can shift this behavior:

- Stop Yourself Mid-Thought
  - Gabby Bernstein has a great phrase she talks about when she catches herself in judgment- she says *"wait, why am I talking?"* Similar to rewiring our thoughts, this is just a pattern that we can break with practice and awareness.

- Bring It Back To Yourself
  - How does this judgment reflect how I judge myself?

- Remind Yourself That You Are Placing an Order for What You're Judging
  - Delete the judgment. "I take it back, Spirit!" Haha.

- Shift Into Celebration
  - "Who does she think she is, driving that car and wearing that outfit at her age?"
    - → She really has so much confidence and owns her desires - it's refreshing to see!

  - "Wow, he needs a lot of attention. How annoying."
    - → I acknowledge his ability to fully express himself, without fear of judgment. If I'm really honest, I admire that.

  - "He makes way too much money for his own good."
    - → It's inspiring that the ability to earn income like that is possible.

We have to shift from low vibrations to high vibrations in order to truly be happy and feel abundance. It's easy to judge others, but it doesn't feel good. We need to remember that the judgment itself repels money from us, as well as stealing much of our precious energy and happiness.

Be honest, do you find yourself judging others a lot? This can be something you say out loud, or just the mean critical human in your head.

What judgments have you made most often about people who earn a lot of money?

What judgments have you made most often about people who do not earn a lot of money?

What judgments have you made about how people spend their money?

How do you think this has affected the amount of money flowing into you?

What are you telling the Universe energetically with this vibration?

The truth is that much of the time, the way we are judging others is just a reflection of how we judge ourselves and how cruel we are to ourselves. We spoke earlier about how speaking poorly about ourselves is a huge leak of our energy, but it's so common it's worth looking at again here through a different lens.

How often do you find yourself in self-judgment?

Where do you judge yourself the most?

What do you say to yourself?

Does this correlate at all with where you are most judgmental with others?

Are these judgments you make about yourself helpful in any way?

How could you shift these judgments to positive affirmations?

You can admire someone else without questioning your own worth.

#SacredWealth

ABUNDANCE PRINCIPLE 24: STOP THE COMPARISON GAME

Comparing yourself to others hurts your heart. We are each individually perfect in our creation and when we compare to someone else and misperceive that they are "better" than us in some way - it's like directly insulting the angels.

It's easy to get into comparison mode in the age we live in today with constant access to seeing others on their best days , or with a filter covering up a bad day. We have to develop the practice of staying in our own lane. Everyone is operating on a different timeline.

You might see the random girl on Instagram, who seems to have everything: the hot husband, perfect body, cute kids, fancy house, and luxe everything - but you don't see what happens behind the scenes after the photo is taken. Is it all staged? Is it real? How are her actual interactions with her husband? Does she spend much time with him? Does she like her life? You don't know.

You might see your mentor slaying the game, but you don't actually know what that life is like behind the scenes. How is the work/life balance? Is she happy with her life? You don't know. How much time does she get to herself? How often is she glued to her phone or her obligations? Is she actually experiencing the freedom you think she is?

We can't ever really know, so let's just stop thinking that the grass is greener over there, when that person could be dying their grass green and everyone thinks it's the prettiest grass in all of the land. So much is unseen that it is absolutely just ridiculous to think anyone's life is grander than our own. Go listen to that song by J.Cole "Love Yourz."

I think if we were sitting up in God's chair and we saw how everyone compares themselves with others, we'd just roll our eyes and gracefully say "how can you still be missing your own grand divinity?"

In what ways do you compare yourself to others?

181

What areas do you find yourself comparing most?

```



```

Why do you think that is?

```



```

If you are having trouble with comparison, just take the bait away. It's easy to "mute" or unfollow people online. **Why subject yourself to anything on your social media feed that doesn't make you feel inspired or bring you joy?** Who we are following is a choice.

If the person you are comparing yourself to is in your life, we can't always just get them out of our lives. For example, if your best friend is ultra beautiful and successful and you catch yourself in comparison, what you can choose to do is allow what you're comparing to become an inspiration and admiration instead of something negative. So take your friend's beauty and success, and say "wow, this really inspires me. What could I do to create a feeling of more success in myself? How could I tap into that same energy?" Don't even bring the other person into it, because they have nothing to do with it! Easier said than done sometimes, I know. Practice makes perfect.

Most importantly, we must address the underlying issue that is behind comparison to begin with : the belief that we aren't perfect, exactly as we are, in this moment.

We can only see things in others if there is a seed of it in ourselves. You can only recognize someone else's beautiful artwork if you, too, have that seed of creativity within. You can only recognize someone else's work ethic if you have the capability to work that hard as well. So instead of thinking "I'll never be as beautiful as her", shift your thought to gratitude and appreciation - *"thank you for showing me the beauty I know is already within me."* Replace the word "beauty" and Insert whatever you typically compare yourself about with others.

What we've learned about vibrational attraction so far reminds us that if we are focusing on how ___ someone else is (from a point of comparison), it implies to the Universe that we don't have that, and the Universe always listens. When we shift to gratitude and focus on appreciating what we know is within us, the Universe listens to that, too. Comparison is never a good use of our energy and sends the opposite directions to the Universe than we would like.

Say it with me: I am exactly where I'm meant to be and am perfect as I am right now. I promise to stay in my own lane. Everyone is on a different part of their path.

Name one person or trait that you find yourself comparing yourself to..

What is your comparison acknowledging in that person? (Understanding that you already have this within yourself, as well).

How could you shift your judgment and comparison into gratitude and appreciation?

What action could you take that would take you out of comparison and into creation (or further appreciation) of the trait you're acknowledging this person for?

Forgiveness is choosing yourself and your own happiness over poisoning yourself and carrying the pain.

#SacredWealth

ABUNDANCE PRINCIPLE 25: RELEASE RESENTMENT + FORGIVE

Similar to judgment, resentment is total poison in our bodies. Resentment is a persistent feeling of bitterness that we hold towards someone or something. It's a lingering anger that won't go away. A feeling of hate that we're carrying. The problem is - we are the ones carrying it. Not the person that it is directed at.

Resentment can be slow-growing or can result from one incident. For example, someone in a relationship could develop resentment over years of feeling neglected or abandoned, while the other person's career thrives. Someone could build a slow-growing resentment that their needs aren't being met in their relationship and hold bitterness towards their partner. Resentment towards a parent could grow over years from one sibling feeling like they didn't get the same attention as another sibling. Or, resentment could come from a single incident, like a partner cheating on their spouse, a parent saying something rude to their child in front of others, etc.

You may have heard this story before that teaches us about how dangerous resentment can be - imagine a snake is just slithering along on it's path and it sees a shiny knife. Thinking that this blade is a predator on it's way to attack, the snake attacks first and even though it hurts, he keeps squeezing the knife. All along, he's squeezing the blade into his own skin, hurting himself as he chooses to continue squeezing. This is what we do when we hold a grudge or hold resentment for others.

Resentment only creates suffering for ourselves - the other person or situation that holding resentment for is affected energetically, but on a conscious level, they aren't really impacted. Only you are. Only your level of happiness is affected. Only your heart has that extra layer of walls up.

I hope this makes you laugh. There was someone years ago that I held massive resentment towards. Thinking about this person would make my blood boil and any shred of a good mood would disappear. Thoughts would always pop up about the situation when I was at work, so trying to move the energy out of my body, I would go for a break and walk around the lake by my office. Good plan. However, the mistake that I made was choosing to listen to the Beyonce song "Ring the Alarm" on repeat for my whole walk, getting myself more and more and more worked up with each listen. Our thoughts are so powerful, remember? So as I'm listening to the lyrics, getting myself angrier and angrier, I was also building up new thoughts and stories in my head that solidified MY VERSION of what happened, creating more poisonous energy in my body that was definitely exaggerated truths. This had to be a funny scene to any people who passed me, or God forbid, to my co-workers if they could see me out of their office windows. Just imagine seeing a 24 year old girl power walking around the lake in a tight little professional dress and flats, sweating bullets, with a look of pure rage plus the sass and attitude of Beyonce - what a catch.

Those walks never made me feel better. In fact, I had a lot more moments where I experienced those very same feelings after I began my walks - my vibration was attracting more of it. When we work ourselves up like this, we are re-creating the trauma that existed initially and then diving back into that energy and vibration over and over again. Instead of choosing to move forward, we choose to just go back into the anger created by the experience. We also do this through talking and talking and talking about the event a million times with our friends. Insert that friend who is still talking about her breakup from 2 years ago, but as a friend, you've allowed her to keep talking about it even when you know it's no longer a healthy release of energy - it's reliving it unnecessarily.

Letting go of resentment is in no way easy - it requires massive self -love and the ability to get vulnerable. In this section's work, we are going to address some of the top resentments taking up precious space in your body and how they are impacting you, your abundance and your ability to attract what you desire. In the next principle, I'll show you how you can move through your resentments, release that energy and move into a new understanding.

Name 3 people or situations that you are holding resentment against - and why:

How does this resentment impact your daily life?

How does it impact you when you think about these individuals? How do you feel about them? How has it affected your relationship with them currently (if you are still in relationship with them)?

How has this resentment affected your life and your relationships, outside of your relationship with these particular individuals you've chosen?

What do you think this resentment is doing to your vibration? What are you asking for if you are vibrating at this frequency?

Forgiveness is the only way that we can truly move beyond resentment and release that poison from our hearts. I wasn't ever taught how to truly forgive someone. I wasn't taught how to forgive, period. The way I knew to forgive someone was to tell myself "I'm letting this go..." but then I would still think about it in the back of my head. I wouldn't really let it go. I wanted to, I just didn't know how.

Just like resentment, holding grudges and not fully forgiving causes us more pain than the other person or situation. Relating this to abundance, this energy just takes up massive room where we could be allowing more magic, wealth, happiness or joy in. We want to clear this so that we can be happier humans and feel more alive with life.

Forgiveness doesn't mean that you are condoning what someone did, that someone else didn't mess up, that the situation wasn't uncalled for, or that you are saying "it's ok" to the betrayal or unkind act. Forgiveness is choosing yourself and your own happiness over carrying pain. Forgiveness means that you love yourself enough to let the pain that isn't serving you go.

Before we get started with the activity that will support you in releasing this I want you to think of 20 things you can forgive. You have them in you. This could be forgiving the person who told you that you had buck teeth in 5th grade to the person who betrayed you that hurt the most. List 20 things you're ready to release. Try to think of items other than the resentments you listed already. Go.

| 1. |
| 2. |
| 3. |
| 4. |
| 5. |
| 6. |
| 7. |
| 8. |
| 9. |
| 10. |
| 11. |
| 12. |
| 13. |
| 14. |
| 15. |
| 16. |
| 17. |
| 18. |
| 19. |
| 20. |

One of my top 5 favorite personal development books is called "Radical Forgiveness" by Colin Tipping and I highly suggest you purchase it. It should be required reading for all humans, in my opinion. It's a book that will change your life and support you over and over again when you need a reminder of how you can truly let go. In the back of this book, Tipping provides a worksheet that you can use to help you through individual instances where you want to forgive someone. I am not even lying when I say I've probably done this worksheet 35 times (if not more). When I went to go download the worksheet again from the website, Google said "you have visited this webpage many times." I told you!

I'm going to share the short version of this process below so that we can work through at least one area of forgiveness together, but I recommend that you download the full worksheet and print it out (maybe a few copies) so you can go through the entire process in a more granular way. If you'd like to download a copy, I've included the full worksheet in the Book Resources section at www.AlyWilkins.Me.

For some situations, you will go through this forgiveness process once and you're all wiped clean of the incident or event. For other situations, you may need to go through this 3, 30 or 300 times. It's all perfect. Just have the intention that you want to clear yourself.

There have been multiple times that I've gone through this process and then check my phone and I have a text or an email for someone, saying "hey, I'm sorry for XYZ." Don't have that expectation, but know that if it's a person you are forgiving, they will feel this energy in some way. Energy is within everything.

General *Radical Forgiveness* Process:
  1. Tell the story from your point of view
  2. Feel your feelings.
  3. Collapse the story.
  4. Reframe the story.
  5. Integrate the shift.

Let's dive into the nitty gritty parts of the *Radical Forgiveness* process.

1. **Let yourself be the victim.** Let yourself spill everything out - all the ugly, dramatic feelings regarding what happened.

2. **Acknowledge why you are upset** with someone and how their actions made you feel.

3. **Remind yourself of your humanity.** We are humans - not emotionless robots - and we get to acknowledge that we are entitled to our feelings! We don't judge ourselves for having feelings. Then we must remind ourselves that no one else can ever make us feel a certain way. Our feelings are ours and we choose them (even if it doesn't always seem that way). We are always ultimately choosing our reactions.

4. **Get real and acknowledge that you want someone else to change** in order to show up for you in the perfect way you'd like them to. It's acknowledging that we may have expectations of others and when they don't meet them, we view them as less than perfect. We have to get clear on the judgments, expectations and behaviors that show us that we wanted this person to change their ways to align with what works for us, instead of what works for them.

5. **What are the facts?** Get clear on the true story. Act as if a third party neutral observer was watching from a distance and telling you what happened. If you're like me, you can tend to over dramatize things (especially over time) and sometimes the facts of the situation can become muddled under the exaggerations that you may have added that make the incident seem much worse.

6. **What did you make up about the event?** What interpretations did you make from the story? How emotionally attached did you get to these interpretations?

7. **Do the interpretations you made from this event correlate with a core wound you have?** Does it align with another negative story you have about yourself or with the world? Where else have similar issues occurred? Is this a pattern?

8. **Reframe how you see this event happening.**

9. **What have you learned about this?**

Let's look at an example before you use this process with something happening in your own life. I'm going to give you an intense example, but unfortunately one that many people face. When you use your own forgiveness practice, know that again *anything that causes you a disturbance is worthwhile.* I just want to show you an intense example so that you can see how we can forgive even in difficult situations.

Imagine that Mike and Jen have been married for 4 years, and Mike starts to get a weird feeling about his marriage with Jen. She starts pulling away and seeming more distracted. She's not acting like she has before. He confronts her one afternoon, asking her what's wrong and what's going on with her. Jen tells him that she has been having an affair and has been speaking with a divorce lawyer. Here is an example of what Mike's forgiveness process could look like. This would be an example where one would likely need to go through the forgiveness process several times.

1. Let yourself be the victim.	How could Jen hurt me like this? Why would she have married me if she wasn't in love with me? What did he offer her that I didn't? I bought her the house she wanted, let her decorate everything in her favorite designs, do everything that she has asked. I thought we had a great marriage. We never fought. Where did I go wrong? How could I miss something so huge? She says it had nothing to do with me and it's out of her control how she feels about this other guy, but.... We are married! Does that mean nothing to you? .... Continue for 14 pages if necessary.
2. Acknowledge why you're upset and how their actions made you feel.	Jen, I'm horrified that you broke our vows. I'm furious that you lied to me over and over again. I'm deeply sad that you broke my heart and betrayed me. You made me feel worthless, useless and stupid. I feel like I can't trust anyone ever again.
3. Remind yourself of your humanity and willingness to acknowledge and accept your feelings.	I'm human and I acknowledge that my feelings are valid! I'm allowed to have my feelings. I acknowledge that I'm responsible for how I react to everything. How I react has nothing to do with Jen and what I'm upset with her about. My reactions are my own.
4. Get clear on the judgments, expectations and behaviors that show us that we wanted this person to change.	I wanted Jen to be a "good wife" and honor her commitments to me that she made when we chose to get married. I wanted Jen to talk to me if something was wrong in our relationship so that I could have had a chance to fix this. I wanted Jen to break up with this guy because I know that we belong together. I wanted Jen to cut things off with this person and come back to me. We could deal with the aftermath of the hurt from there. I wanted her first step to be breaking up with her boyfriend, instead of breaking up with me, her husband.

5.	What are the facts?	Jen cheated on me. Jen broke our vows. Jen tried to talk to me a few years ago about how she wasn't getting her needs met. I told her we'd go on a couple's trip that we never went on. Jen asked us to go to counseling, but my work schedule was too heavy. Jen always complained that I didn't make enough time for her.
6.	What did I make up about this event? What interpretations did I make about the story?	I made up that I am unloveable. I made up that I can't trust other people. I made up that Jen isn't trustworthy. I made up that marriage never works. I made up that I am a bad husband.
7.	Do the interpretations you made from this event correlate with a core wound you have?	I always felt like I was a bad husband because Jen was constantly telling me that I wasn't doing ____ right or wasn't giving her enough _____. My mother said similar things to me growing up. I wasn't helping enough, I wasn't around enough, etc.
8.	Reframe the story.	Jen cheated on me and broke our vows, but she did try for years to get me to go to therapy with her and work on our communication problems. I always prioritized work, since that paid for our lavish lifestyle, and told her we'd make it happen the next month (and never did). She did give me warnings, I just wasn't paying close enough attention. She shouldn't have lied or been sneaking around behind my back, but if I wasn't giving her love, knowing what a prize she is, of course someone else is going to see that and claim it for themselves. I wish she would have talked to me right when it happened, but she tried to talk to me so often beforehand, she may have thought it would be a lost cause. I know her soul and she is a good person. I'm sure that this tore her apart as well. That being said, I'm still allowed to be upset about this for now, but I want to forgive her. I don't want to carry this resentment and anger towards her because it will affect my future if I do so.
9.	What did you learn from this experience?	I learned that I must consider my priorities carefully and become a better communicator in my relationships. I learned, after talking with Jen openly about it, that this was extremely hard for her and she had been sick for months, trying to decide

	what to do. She was hurt for years that I wasn't willing to meet her halfway in our relationship and prioritized myself over others. I learned that in my next relationship, I will make communication a priority.

See how this process shifted? This is a hard thing to forgive, but if Mike didn't forgive Jen, what would his future look like? Would he carry a distrusting energy into all of his future relationships? Would he even be able to get vulnerable enough again to have another relationship? He could choose to just be angry with Jen forever and not learn the lesson, but then he would be missing a very important learning lesson and key for his growth.

Now, it's your turn. Answer the questions below in regards to a situation you're holding onto and having trouble letting go of.

What is one thing you're holding onto that you're upset with someone over? What's the story you're telling yourself about this? Get into your real feelings - lay them out.

Who are you upset with and how did their actions make you feel?

Acknowledge your human-ness.

- ❏ I am entitled to my feelings.
- ❏ I don't judge myself for having feelings and emotions about this.
- ❏ I don't judge how I feel about this situation.
- ❏ No one else can make me feel a certain way.
- ❏ I choose how I react to situations.

What expectations did you have of this person that you are upset with? What behaviors did you want them to exhibit?

What are the objective facts of the situation?

What interpretations did you make from this event?

Do these interpretations correlate with a wounded belief that you have somewhere else in life? Is this a pattern?

Where did you learn this belief? Is it ultimately true?

How could you reframe this story?

What have you learned about this?

Great work. I highly recommend that you print out the full worksheet (and purchase Radical Forgiveness) to forgive at an even deeper level. Again, you can download the full workbook at the Book Resources area of my website www.AlyWilkins.Me.

Give from a place of love and joy.

#SacredWealth

ABUNDANCE PRINCIPLE 26: PRACTICE GIVING + RECEIVING

One of the ways we can receive a great amount of abundance is through giving. When you give, the Universe hears "I have more than enough!" and will continue giving you more than enough. We don't give from the intention to receive more, but that is an added perk!

Have you ever given your time, kindness or money and not felt joy? If you watched Friends, you might remember the episode where Joey and Phoebe are having a debate on if there are any truly unselfish good deeds. Joey thinks that any time you give, you get something in return so you are ultimately doing it "selfishly." Phoebe thinks she can prove him wrong. Throughout the whole episode, she tries to do all of these good deeds and ALL of them bring her joy in some way. When we give, we receive so much in return!

In order to feel truly abundant, only give when it comes from love. Sometimes we may feel obligated to give, but then it may not feel so good. Sometimes people give in order to receive acknowledgement or praise, or even so that they can share about it and keep up a certain appearance. Those aren't the ways that giving will attract abundance.

Giving feels good when it comes from the heart. The additional perk is that when we give from love, we receive it back tenfold! Often we think that giving has to come in the form of monetary donations - but there are so many other ways we can give that don't cost much at all (or anything):

- Sharing kindness and compassion
- Giving a compliment to someone
- Checking on someone via text or call
- Donate something you don't need anymore to someone who will appreciate it
- Park further away with the intention that someone who needs to park closer can have that space
- Use Amazon Smile so that a portion of your purchase goes to a charity
- Pray for someone without telling them
- Share a local business that you love (they will appreciate it!)
- Texting a friend a voice note reminding them how powerful and amazing they are
- Mailing a letter that will bring a smile to someone
- Bringing a gift to someone's home
- Offer to babysit for your friend who is overloaded with her kids and work
- Make a larger portion of dinner and bring it to a friend
- Donate your valuable time to something you care about
- Help a friend with something important to them
- Smile at someone (a smile from a stranger can make a big difference)

When we give, we want to give from a place of pure joy. That's where the true magic is.

What would make you feel really excited to support someone else in?

In what ways could you easily give that don't cost any money?

Do you feel called to give in any ways financially to people or causes you care about?

How could you remind yourself to give more or to do this on a daily basis?

Just setting the intention that you want to give more and serve through your love and energy will create the opportunities and the reminders for you!

OPEN YOUR ARMS TO RECEIVE

Often we have abundance pouring into our lives, but we aren't able to see it or actually receive it. Peta Kelly uses the reference of alignment being like a garden hose in her book, *Earth is Hiring*. If there's a big fat kink in your hose (if you're stepping on it), you're blocking the flow! Once you unfold the hose, abundance will pour out.

Let's talk about a few ways you may be blocking yourself from receiving what's wanting to come through to you in the physical:

Take Off The Blindfold

First off, you just aren't seeing some of the things coming to you. You know when you're going to go get something at the grocery store and you find a coupon for 20% off? Or when you are going to get coffee before work but your friend texts you and says "picking up coffee. What do you want?" Or when you were seriously running low on snacks and your mom sends you a care package with a bunch of your favorite snacks? We are already manifesting a lot in terms of discounts, savings, free stuff, etc that we just aren't paying attention to. When we look at it all in bulk, we're usually surprised at how much is already pouring through. Money is like, "SEE?! I support you so much already - would you give me some credit FOR ONCE!" *dramatic backbend*

The first thing to do to see the magic already flowing into your life is to start tracking the amount of abundance coming into your life. We tend to be tunnel visioned and only think about something coming in a certain way and don't see the big picture. If you actually tracked the amount of things coming into your life to support you, you'd see how abundant you are!

For the next week, I want you to track everything that comes to you as a surprise, discounts, free samples, gifts, coupons, buy one/get one deals for things you were already going to buy, etc. Add everything. **Keep track of what you are attracting here:**

199

Receiving Gifts + Surprise Purchases

It's really interesting how sometimes we are so uncomfortable with receiving gifts or money. We have to understand that if someone offers you something, it probably gives them some amount of joy to do so. Gifts are my personal love language and when I give someone something, it genuinely gives me as much joy as receiving gifts on my end. It makes me happy to give someone else a gift. So, if someone offers you a gift of some kind, allow yourself to receive it (if you want it).

How open are you to receiving gifts?

How do you respond when someone offers to buy you something or pay for something that you were going to buy?

What comes up for you when they ask? Are you excited or uncomfortable?

Another way to tune into this - how would you feel if I gave you $1,000? Are you excited or uncomfortable? What if I made it $10,000 or $10 million, with no strings attached?

If this makes you uncomfortable, why do you think that is? What belief is underlying that feeling of being uncomfortable? Examples: I am not worthy, I didn't earn it, I don't want to owe you, I'm not deserving - (all untrue and lies).

```



```

Compliments, Affection + Nice Gestures

Some people are super uncomfortable with compliments. They deflect them like they have a superhero shield.

- "Your shirt is so pretty!" -- "Thanks, it was 50% off" ..... ***They didn't ask for the price.***

- "Your eye color is so gorgeous" -- "it's actually really common, everyone in my family has this color eyes"....... ***would you just accept your beauty?***

- "I love your style" -- " I just get tons of ideas from Pinterest." *We've all seen the pinterest fails....* ***Just accept that you have great style and say thank you.***

Notice how often we need to explain or describe something when we get complimented. Practice just saying thank you - and leaving it at that. Allow yourself to absorb the compliment.

Are you awkward af when people compliment you? Do you find that you typically deflect compliments?

```



```

Do you feel the need to elaborate on something when you get a compliment? Why?

```



```

Get Present to Receive Valuable Energy

Receiving energy is a big part of our ability to receive. Are you able to be present?

Think about the last time you went to dinner with a friend. Were you truly present with them? Or were you checking your phone throughout the conversation? Receiving your friend's energy could be super valuable for you - your conversation and your experience could go much deeper when you're able to be present with them.

How could you be more present in your life? Where do you find yourself distracted or not fully giving your energy to others when you spend time with them?

Allow Help + Ask For It!

It's funny because sometimes you could really use help with something, but when someone offers, you're like "oh you're so sweet, I appreciate it but I got it. I'm good. Thanks though." And then you struggle through the thing that could have been much easier with your friend's help or support. Do you catch yourself doing this ever?

In the same vain, a lot of us have a hard time asking for help from others. It can feel excruciating for the ego. But why? People are often happy to help us out with something. I've experienced this on airplanes a lot. My carry-on is usually 9,000 pounds and I used to try to use all of my strength to put it up in the overhead compartment, almost crushing all of the people underneath it and getting a lot of scared looks. Eventually, I got sick of breaking my back to try to push up my 37 books that I had to bring for my 4-day trip and I started asking others to help. Usually, when I ask, people are more than happy to help. The people underneath my overhead compartments usually feel a lot safer, too.

How do you normally respond when people offer help to you? Do you accept their help?

Do you ask for help when you need it? Do you notice you try to power through on your own, or are you open to the help?

What in your life could you use some extra help with now? Who could help you? What comes up for you when you think about asking them for help?

Where do you not allow yourself to get help because you think you can do it better?

It isn't all up to us. When we allow ourselves to receive the help that is already there (but we likely aren't seeing), life gets a lot easier and we can become so much more aware of the abundance and support that we have right in front of us.

"We don't stop playing
because we grow old;
we grow old because
we stop playing."

GEORGE BERNARD SHAW

#SacredWealth

ABUNDANCE PRINCIPLE 27: ACTIVATE YOUR CHILD LIKE SPIRIT + PLAY!

We've been taught this huge misconception that adults need to be serious. There are times when being serious can support us, but most of the time, adding fun and play into something will always improve the experience.

The real magic in life is in our childlike essence - that curiosity, wonder, joyful, silly, playful spirit. Children allow themselves to play and just have fun. They are so open-minded. They let themselves explore and use their imagination wildly. Children aren't afraid to tell people that they love them. Children don't show much fear at all. They just act on their excitement.

When we are growing up, we either want to become adults so badly (think about teenage girls today, looking like they are 25) or we are forced to become adults too soon when our childhood is taken away from us too soon. We don't get to experience that purely childlike spirit nearly long enough. Once we are actually adults, we have this tendency of letting everything be so serious. All of the sudden we are burdened with so much responsibility that comes with trying to keep ourselves alive and taking care of all of our adult-y duties.

Think about someone you know who is just full of light. They radiate. When you walk into a room, they lighten it up. That person is likely very light-hearted, playful and brings fun into everything they do. Everyone usually loves that person - but most importantly, that person probably has a really amazing quality of life.

I'm really lucky because I've had a great example of keeping your child-like spirit throughout my life, from my Dad. He finds a million things to laugh at everyday. Here's a perfect example - my mom used to host different family gatherings and parties for family friends and neighbors. My dad bought a fart machine, which was his favorite toy of all time. He would keep the remote in his pocket and put the fart machine in the bathroom downstairs that guests used with the volume on loud. While my Grandma was in the bathroom, he would turn it on and light it up. It would make EVERYONE laugh. He is constantly pulling pranks and telling jokes. You'll hear him laughing in the other room, by himself, at something he found on the internet, everyday.

My sister is the same way. The other day she texted me a photo and said "I'm just waiting for my husband to spot this." She had put two googly eye stickers on a framed photo of her daughter on the wall. It was hilarious and made both of us laugh. My sister will consistently send me hilarious photos of her (that I save for future blackmail) , or when I'm with her, she'll steal my phone and I'll find it later and see selfies of her with grapes in her upper lip, looking like a chipmunk. Life is supposed to be fun - not serious.

We need more moments of joy in our lives! Where we can just act silly, playful and make our hearts light up. We can easily start to implement more of these moments in our lives with intention. While you're cooking dinner for your family of 79, try listening to your favorite music instead of letting yourself get stressed thinking about everything you still have left to do before bed. Dance in front of the refrigerator while you're finding your late night snack instead of just standing there. Make yourself laugh at any opportunity available.

A few years ago, I was sitting at my cubicle and spending most of my day in pure seriousness while I was at work. While I was pretending to put 100% of my focus on work, but really was watching a video from Peta Kelly (one of my favorites, obviously) in the tabs hidden behind my main computer screen, I heard her ask **"How can you make your everyday activities 5% more fun?"** I wrote it on a Post-It note and put "5%" on my computer, so my colleagues wouldn't know what it was referring to. 5% really isn't that much. It's not completely changing the activity. Just making it a tiny bit more fun.

At that very moment, I was creating a social media analytics report (which I absolutely hated doing, it was like pulling hairs out of my head one by one) and I thought that was the perfect opportunity to try to make it a little bit more fun. I had to make those reports for an entire week every single month, so I might as well try to enjoy it a little. First, I just started adding color to the Excel sheets. Scandalous, I know. Then I started writing the reports with a little more pizzazz. I'd add in funny remarks that would make my clients laugh. I wouldn't do that now for fun, but it made a huge part of my job much more enjoyable as I implemented that 5% rule everytime I worked on those reports.

I started implementing this question in my life everywhere - and it made a HUGE difference!

> *How can I make this 5% more fun?* - Peta Kelly

On a scale of 1-10, how serious do you think you are?

On a scale of 1-10, how much do you let yourself play?

How could you make your everyday activities just a little bit more fun? Just 5%?

Do yourself a favor and write "5%" on a post-it note and put it somewhere you'll see it everyday.

A way we can easily play more is starting to do the things we love to do a lot more often! It's easy to get bogged down with being a "responsible adult" (BORING) and feel like we don't have enough time for the things we love. We have more than enough time.

What really brings you joy?

What are some things you loved doing as a child?

What are things you'd love to do that you haven't done for some reason?

Go do them! Put them on your calendar.

ENERGY HEALING: FILLING UP THE HEART CHAKRA

In an effort to protect our hearts from pain, we tend to close up and build walls quite often, which doesn't allow us to experience true unconditional love. These healing tools will help support you in opening your heart in a way that feels safe for you. By being more open and vulnerable, we are able to fully experience all of the abundance life has to offer. When you feel like you're starting to tighten up and protect your heart, utilize these tools to help open you back up.

Visualization:

Imagine that you're laying in a large green field of grass. You can feel the ground underneath you, holding you up completely. Feel your fingers touching the dewy, cool grass and the grass underneath your feet. Breathe in and smell the fresh air. Noticing the feeling of warmth from the sun and the wind on your face.

Placing your hand on your heart, imagine that there is a small green orb in your heartspace, the size of a marble. Imagine this sparkling green light expanding larger and larger, until it fills your entire chest and torso area. Notice how this feels in your body. Feel tension dissolve and an overwhelming sense of unconditional love takes over you. Imagine this light slowly expanding beyond your body, beyond the green grassy field, beyond the city and even the state you are in. Keep going as far as you'd like!

Physical Tools and Support:

- Allow yourself to go through your day with your chest lifted and shoulders back. Notice when you shrink or collapse in this area. There are many heart opening yoga practices that you can find online that can support you here!
- Keep roses around! Roses help us embody the physical opening of the heart. Imagine your heart blooming open just like the rose does. Once the rose petals dry up, I love to put them in the bathtub instead of just throwing them away, so I can fully utilize the plant in all forms.
- Physically tap on your heartspace when you feel yourself tightening up.
- Read the book "Radical Forgiveness" by Colin Tipping.

Heart Chakra Affirmations:

- I allow myself to feel nurtured and held.
- I receive the love that is available to me.
- It is safe for me to feel my emotions deeply.
- I allow myself to lower my walls of protection. I am safe.

- I choose to forgive and let go.
- I allow myself to be vulnerable in this moment.
- I fearlessly open my heart and allow myself to receive.

Heart Chakra Crystals:

- Top Recommendation: Rose Quartz for self-love and unconditional love
- Jade to attract love and abundance
- Malachite for balancing, clearing and transformation
- Green calcite for healing and compassion
- Any crystals that are pink or green!

Heart Chakra Essential Oils:

I prefer to put these oils straight on my heart area (with a carrier oil), rub them between my hands and breathe them in or diffuse them.

- Neroli to create harmony and uplift your spirit
- Rose oil to open and feel unconditional love
- Lavender oil to help calm the nerves
- Marjoram for support with grief
- Jasmine for hope and happiness
- Doterra offers a "Forgive" oil that is wonderful!

Throat Chakra

Viśuddha

Throat Chakra

Throat —

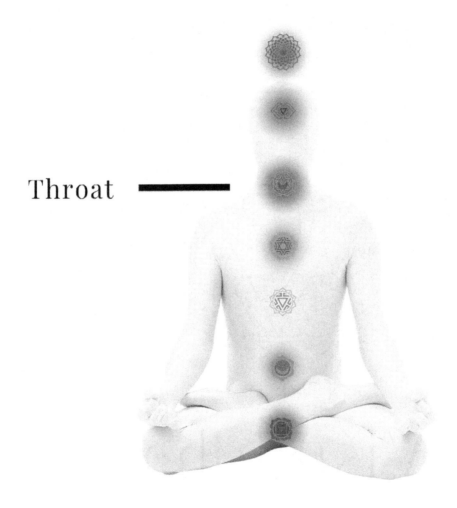

THROAT CHAKRA : VISHUDDHA

The Throat Chakra is located right at the throat, governing our thyroid, throat, mouth and neck and shoulder area. This energy wheel is all about healthy expression of yourself. Sharing your voice loudly and truthfully with love. When our Throat Chakra is expressing itself in a healthy way, we can clearly communicate what we need and desire from life and communicate in our relationships in a way that everyone is respected and understood.

When the Throat Chakra is imbalanced, we are usually either under expressing ourselves, expressing in an inauthentic way or can even be saying too much. Inauthentic expression can include using your words as a means of manipulation, to gossip, to spread negativity or fear, or expressing a false or dimmed down version of yourself. Physically, this can show up in the body through common ailments such as constant sore throats, dental problems, thyroid issues, or neck and upper back pain.

To keep this area healthy and in balance, we want to prioritize being true to ourselves and expressing ourselves authentically. That starts with getting to know who we really are authentically, underneath all of the masks and conditioning that we've been living in most of our lives. Even more so than that, living in a way that's in line with our values. We want to speak with confidence and power.

In regards to abundance, the Throat Chakra helps us effectively express our truth so we can speak and attract what we desire to us, through our language and authenticity.

Our words are like spells - we must use them wisely.

#SacredWealth

ABUNDANCE PRINCIPLE 28 : WATCH YOUR LANGUAGE

We've already talked about how the Universe listens to our thoughts, behaviors and actions in order to deliver that same energy back to us. What we physically voice is literally like a spell - what we allow ourselves to say out loud holds even more weight than our thoughts do. So, let's take a quick look at some of the common ways we limit ourselves through our words:

- Using absolutes like **"always"**, **"never"** or **"everytime"** - these words are giving further directions for the Universe to follow. They must be used extremely wisely!

- Limiting words such as **"can't"** or **"don't know how"** - these are just disempowering! We can do anything that we set our mind to, but we don't always want to. Using this verbiage can be an easy way out if we just don't want to do something. To create a more empowering vibration, you can shift to "I choose to get support with this" or "This seems complicated, but I know I can figure it out with help."

- Saying **"should"** usually means we don't want to, but feel obligated. If you don't want to do the thing, don't do it. If you want to do it, choose to do it. "Should" is disempowering, especially when we tell others they "should" do something.

- Making judgments like **"good" or "bad"** keeps us limited in a box with black and white thinking. Nothing is inherently good or bad - it's just our perception of it. Us judging anything as "good" or "bad" limits our experience and creates more judgment (the abundance sucker).

- **"Too expensive"** - It's not about the price, it's about our priorities. Travel is my priority, so to me, spending a lot on a car payment is "too expensive", but someone else who values their car more would think that my trip to Bali was "too expensive". If my health is my priority, then buying the real fruit juice is not expensive. The concentrated juice that's made of fake everything costs me a lot more in the long run. If your priority is fashion over everything, then the $1,200 Louis Vuitton purse might be worth you sacrificing all of your other spending money that month. It's not too expensive, it's just not your priority. Let's be clear.

All of these language shifts are huge - we're taught to speak this way! Start to become aware of how often you actually use each of these words.

Which of these words do you find yourself saying most in regards to money and finances?

What do you think you "should" be doing in regards to money and finances?

What do you judge as being "good" or "bad" in regards to money and finances?

Just by looking at your language, what are you asking the Universe to deliver to you?

We have to realize how powerful our words are. We say a lot about money without even being aware of it. We talk about money with friends, family and people we trust, and often have unspoken agreements and stories about money. For example : you might constantly talk with your family about how you never have money ,or how you need to save more money, or how everything is so expensive, or how it's so unfair how certain people have more money - insert whatever your family stories are here.

What do you catch yourself saying about money to yourself?

What do most of your conversations about money center around with other people?

What are some of the storylines that you talk about with your family and friends? List at least 5 that come to mind.

What is the experience of physical money among those around you? Does that reflect the way that they talk about money?

Whenever you catch yourself talking about money in a limiting way - stop yourself. Ask yourself - is this what I'm wanting to create?

I Am Affirmations

The phrase "I am" is powerful and we have to make sure we're using it effectively. When we say "I am", we are affirming directly to the Universe, who will follow through for us.

I want you to start getting aware of what follows those words. For the next few days, start tracking the thoughts that pop in your head that come after "I am." For example : when you make a mistake, what do you say about yourself? When you look in the mirror when you're getting ready for a night out, what do you say about yourself then?

What are the words you say most about yourself in the "I am" framework?

Keep track of this over the next week and I'd like you to put a tally mark next to each time you say the same word to describe yourself. This will show you how often you're giving the Universe instructions in this manner.

We can utilize I am statements to help support us in our growth journey and in our journey to experiencing more abundance on a daily basis.

For example, if you are working on feeling more supported and guided in your life, you can use an affirmation like "I am deeply supported and guided."

We want to make sure that we actually believe the "I Am" statement - so, if you deeply believe that you are broke, using an affirmation like "I am a millionaire" isn't going to be a suitable fit. Your subconscious will immediately reject it and the statement won't do its job. In that case, adding a few additional words like "I am open to believing that I could be a millionaire one day" would be more appropriate. Do a quick check in to make sure that you actually buy what you are repeating to yourself, otherwise, it's a moot point.

These statements are so simple that you may have doubt that they can shift your whole reality.

> **Do not let the simplicity of "I AM" fool you - these are direct instructions to the Universe and your cosmic support team to help guide you to the things, people, places that will support you in creating what you are saying you are.**

You can remind yourself of these affirmations in any ways that works for you - here are a few examples, but trust your intuition and your own creativity if a specific idea is coming to mind:

- Putting Post-It notes around the house in places you will see them daily. You'll want to move these around occasionally so you continue to notice them!
    - Car steering wheel
    - Bathroom mirror
    - Refrigerator / Pantry
    - Office
- Make alarms on your phone with your affirmation as the label.
- Use affirmation apps that will pop up on your phone randomly throughout the day.
- I sometimes create "I AM" vision boards, where I write "I am" in the center and surround the middle piece with my "I am" affirmations or photos that represent the statements.
- Listen to affirmation music or soundtracks.
- Create a morning practice where you write down or speak your affirmations several times. This is a part of my 40 Day Sacred Wealth Ceremony and it has incredible results! Highly effective to reprogram your mind for abundance - it's one of my highest rated programs - check it out at www.AlyWilkins.Me.

Use your creativity here. There is no right or wrong!

For our work here today, we will focus on abundance and re-frame some of your limiting beliefs around finances, wealth or abundance into a new affirmation you can use daily.

Example :

Limiting Belief	Empowering I AM Statement
Finances feel so confusing to me.	I am smart and capable. I am always guided to the resources that support me.
I will never get out of debt.	I am learning how to get out of debt responsibly and am spending in more aligned ways.
Making extra money seems so challenging.	I am always finding creative ways to magnetize more money to me.
I only make money when I work extremely hard.	I am open to learning how I can create more money with ease.

What are a few of the top financial blocks you'd like to shift?

How could you shift this block into an affirmation?

Here is a list of some of my favorite money affirmations to play with:

I am open to creative ways of earning money.	I always have more than enough money.
I attract money with ease.	I am abundant, happy and healthy!
I am always discovering new ways to make money.	I am worthy of all of the money that I receive.
I am open and willing to receive all the wealth life offers me.	I am magnetic and attract everything I desire with ease.
I am at peace with having a lot of money.	I am responsible and handle my money well.
I am creating great impact with my abundance.	I am worthy of having money and wealth.
I am realizing that money comes to me very easily.	I am creating a new experience of money, wealth and abundance like I have never experienced before.
I am a good steward of my money and wealth.	I am a wealthy man/woman/human.
I am highly paid and deliver great value.	I am an abundant being. Abundance is my real Truth.
I am willing to release the stories I have about money that do not serve me.	I am aware of and acknowledge the abundance that comes into my life every single day.
I am worthy of financial freedom.	I am open to receiving financial miracles.
I am learning to trust myself more with making/spending/saving money.	I am always receiving money unexpectedly.
I am creating change in the world with how I spend and invest my money.	I am so thankful for the money I've been given throughout my life.
I am beyond thankful for the luxuries I experience on a daily basis in my life.	I choose how much money I create through my vibration and instructions to the Universe.
I am worthy of receiving money.	I allow myself to receive money, gifts and support.

We vote with our dollar. This is how we create major change.

#SacredWealth

ABUNDANCE PRINCIPLE 29 : PUT YOUR MONEY WHERE YOUR MOUTH IS

Money listens to what we say is important to us and how we are choosing to spend her. Are the two aligned? Money wants to be spent according to your values. She wants to be spent in places that she will give back to things you care about and that you are saying are most important to you right now. How we spend our money is an investment - and we want to make sure our investments align with our values and do not contradict what we are saying is important to us.

For example, do you say that you wish you could travel to a certain place in the world, but "it's just too expensive"? Well, if you stopped buying the $6.99 triple cappuccino macchiato with 14 pumps of caramel every morning, you would have more than enough money for that trip if you just made coffee at home for a year. Money sees that action and then doesn't feel full trust in you. She's like, "um, I'm showing up in the exact amount you need for this trip, but you're spending it on cake pops at Starbucks and complaining to your coffee date that you can't go on the trip because it's too expensive."

Money wants to trust us. It's like if your best friend asked you to borrow money to help get her on her feet after a hard divorce, but then you found out she used your check to buy a snow cone stand. Like, really? This is not what we talked about. You wouldn't really want to give her money after that because you wouldn't trust that she would spend it in the ways she said she would.

What are some things that you've been wanting to do, that you say you can't do because of money, or things that you say you'll do later when you have X amount of money?

Are you aware of any places that money is showing up to help support you with those things you want to do, but you're spending it in other places? Take a look back at the Root Chakra work you did where you tracked your income and saw where there may be some "misaligned" spending.

How could you start applying your resources to the thing you're wanting to do?

___

You Vote With Your Dollar

We vote with our dollar and can create big change this way. For the most part, companies care most about the bottom line. They have to be making money. They have to be profitable in order to survive. Companies will look at the products they are selling and adjust according to what people are buying.

Think about the huge explosion of organic produce, gluten-free foods and vegan options that are now available, compared to 30 years ago. Grocery stores started asking for more of these products because their customers were asking for it. They saw that the demand was there.

It's up to us as the consumer to create demand for the products that create a better world and align with our values. We are the ones in charge so we have to get clear on what's important to us in our investments, no matter how small.

In addition, when we spend our money somewhere, the money trail doesn't stop there. Money just keeps flowing. So what happens to your $34 that you spent at Target on that dress you just had to have? Where does that $34 go? Is a portion of it donated? Does it go to a small business owner? Does $10 of it go to Target's CEO? How much of it goes to support the local community?

These are all things we want to think about. Is our purchase supporting a family sending their daughter to college, or is it helping the CEO buy his 4th Maserati? Don't use this as an opportunity to beat yourself up - it's just about getting clear and doing the best we can.

Here are a few examples of the values I consider when I make purchases:

- I want to support small businesses over big-box retailers as much as possible
- I want to support companies who show they care about my health by using clean ingredients and being honest in their marketing
- I care about animals and don't want them to be exposed to animal testing, so I look for the Cruelty Free label on all beauty products I purchase. This means I purchase almost all of these products online, because unfortunately most everything at big box stores, Ulta, Sephora, etc do not carry cruelty free products (or very many of them).

- I care about how my food is grown so I look for the USDA Organic label on most of the grocery items I purchase
- I want my purchases to be as eco-friendly as possible and will spend more if it uses less plastic, because I recognize that the company is valuing our environment
- I want my purchases to support a cause as often as possible
- I will always purchase from a product or company that is "Rainforest Alliance Certified" over a competitor because I care about protecting the rainforest
- I do not purchase from companies who lie in their marketing! That shows me that they are not trustworthy. Ex: On my last airplane, they were handing out Belvita cookies and the packaging literally said "four hours of steady energy." They are cookies - there is no way that is true. That is manipulation and lying to persuade a purchase and it is sketchy.

What's important to you now when you're making a purchase?

What are some of the values important to you that you'd like to start applying to your purchases?

A lot of this conversation is just about getting educated. We put a lot of faith and trust into the companies we love, but the unfortunate fact is that most companies only care about creating the largest profit - which means that often, they will choose ingredients that are cheaper (and bad for your body), or packaging that harms the environment if it saves them more money. They don't WANT to hurt your body or hurt the environment - but in an attempt to create the largest profits possible, they do whatever they can to save money. Unless the company has deep values, they will do anything to shave costs. The amount of manipulation in marketing is insane.

As a consumer, just to protect ourselves, it's really important that we start to do our research and get educated about the products that we're buying. This is how we can make sure our money is going to places that are really aligned with what's important to us. For example:

- If you don't know that most fruits and vegetables are sprayed with poison, you're not going to care about buying things that are organic. The extra cost won't seem to make sense.
- If you never think about how much money the CEOs of huge companies earn per year, you may never question how much money from your purchase is going towards their 3rd vacation home (and could be directed towards something that aligns more with your personal values)
- If you don't know that 90% of the beauty products are tested on animals, you won't know that your purchase of the most popular shampoo is telling the company that you're ok with them testing on animals.
- If you don't know that artificial coloring is highly toxic and is banned in most of the other countries on the planet, you won't know why you should be looking for foods colored with real fruits and vegetables on the ingredient list.
- If you don't know to look for "paraben-free" shampoo, you won't realize that almost none of the shampoos and conditioners in big-box retailers are caring about your health and safety.

Our purchases, no matter how small, indicate what's important to us. As consumers, it's our duty to make sure our money is going to places that are going to use it well! Even though we aren't physically voicing these purchases, it's an expression of self, which is what the Throat Chakra governs. We can amplify the power of our purchases by sharing the companies that are helping to support our values and change the world in the way we'd like to see it.

What are some rules you could create for yourself when it comes to buying in alignment with your values?

Where are you spending money right now that might be misaligned?

What could you shift spending to that supports your values and what you want to see in the world? Ex: I will start buying Dr. Bronner's toothpaste, so I can support a smaller business, rather than giving my money to Crest. There is no purchase too small to make a difference!

No judgment, just observation. This is something we can check in with often!

What are you holding in? What isn't being said?

#SacredWealth

ABUNDANCE PRINCIPLE 30: SPEAK WHAT NEEDS TO BE SAID

When there is something on our mind that we aren't saying, that can create an imbalance in our throat. Think about your relationships - imagine you are feeling something intense with someone in your life and you have so much you want to tell them, but you choose to just keep it in, instead. You don't tell them. Holding things in is one of the most dangerous things we can do for our health. We don't just angrily blurt out whatever is in our head at the moment, but we do get to honor our feelings and express them when appropriate.

A big energy leakage and area where we can get blocked in the Throat Chakra is through saying things that are not ultimately true for us, or not saying it at all. When we dull down what we really think about something in order to fit in with others or to avoid making a scene, it may not seem harmful, but over time it creates a big imbalance and makes it challenging for us to recognize our Truth when we've been covering it up for so long. Mostly, it just feels bad in our system!

Think about a time that you've needed to talk with someone about something, but waited for some reason. Did you feel a literal lump in your throat form? Did your throat start to get scratchy or get sore the longer you waited? Our bodies are highly intelligent and react to these imbalances.

Do you have a habit of withholding things, or do you freely speak your mind?

Is there anything you're withholding from others?

Is there anything you're not being honest with yourself about?

What fears come up for you when you think about expressing yourself honestly and vulnerably?

```

```

Listen, vulnerable communication is not easy and that's why so many people don't do it. It's easy to not go there because we are afraid of rejection, don't want to create a bigger argument or are fearful of feeling ridiculed. However, the alternative is not being true or honest to yourself, or having to hold that in your body, and that you do not want to do. When we share with someone vulnerably, we want to make sure that we are speaking just from our own experience - not blaming someone, casting judgments or name calling.

Speak purely from your experience and what feels like needs to be expressed, in a way that's truthful, loving and compassionate. Set your intention before you begin this communication so that you know what the purpose of this communication is and think about your ideal response, but have no expectations. We cannot control someone else's reactions - all we can do is express ourselves fully.

Before any big conversation, I like to get out all of my emotional feelings first. I'll write the person a letter (that is just for me) and get out everything. I "squeeze the rag" of all the heightened emotions and try to think about how the communication can be most effective. I think about what my "talking points" are and what is useful to bring up. Often, we just go into blaming or finger pointing and attacking someone is never going to create an open, vulnerable conversation. When we can move past our heightened emotions and come from a calmer place, we will get a lot further. This is NOT easy and is not going to be perfect. We can only try our best to be as neutral as possible before having any big conversations.

Of course, things also happen in the moment, and we have to gauge if we are in the mindset to talk about something in that moment. Personally, I usually need some time to cool down before having big conversations so that I can approach it from a cool place. In your partnerships, you must be honest so that you can create the most effective conversations. If you need space, tell them. If someone tells you they need a 30 minute cool down break, respect it! This doesn't mean "let's talk about this in a year, I don't feel like it right now."

Who is one person you haven't expressed yourself fully to? What do you need to share with them?

How can you say this in a truthful, honest and loving way that expresses yourself in a way you'd be proud of?

What are you looking to receive from this exchange?

Communication is all about practice and the willingness to be open and vulnerable. Be easy on yourself and set yourself up for win/win situations for everyone.

Design your own future and watch it come to fruition.

#SacredWealth

ABUNDANCE PRINCIPLE 31: MAKE A HABIT OF SCRIPTING

Scripting is one of the activities that helps support you in getting really clear about exactly what you want to attract in your life. There is no right or wrong way to write your Script - the only guideline is that it has to be specific! You will be able to envision what you're writing about perfectly. This is one way you can express what excites you in life and what you desire.

You can create scripts for specific areas of your life or for the big picture. We want to write this in a way like it's already happened, so we trick our subconscious mind into creating it! So make sure to write this in past tense. There's no pressure to "get it right" - just think about what you really desire in this now moment and let yourself have fun creating. This should feel fun to write - just allow your creativity to flow and see what comes out! The Universe always delivers this or something better, so you literally cannot mess it up.

Here's an example from my own Financial Script for 5 Years from Now :

Date : August 2025

It is so exciting to me how much abundance flows into my life on a daily basis - abundance of all kinds! The financial abundance in the form of cash makes me feel so supported! I love that I have years worth of savings in my Contingency fund and contribute the maximum amount to my retirement account every year, in addition to purchasing other forms of stock and starting to dip my toes in the real estate market. I love that I wake up in the morning to payment notifications from people who purchased my books overseas overnight and getting weekly emails from Amazon with the hundreds of book copies that have been purchased that week. It's so exciting to watch my profits double every year! I'm not sure what I'm really doing differently, it really just feels like I fall more and more in love with what I do and the way I do it every year. It's been amazing to see that hard work doesn't necessarily correlate to the amount of money I make. When I feel most aligned, I've made the most money and had the most fun creating money. One of my favorite things that I did this year with the abundance of cash that flows into my life was to treat my family to a cruise to the Amalfi coast - my parents, sister and brother-in-law and my partner and I went on an adults cruise where we got to explore Italy and Greece as a treat from me. It was an experience I've always dreamed of doing and it felt so fulfilling to be able to provide such amazing memories for everyone.

Your turn!

In a world where you could create ANYTHING, what would you want in the following areas? Nothing is too much. Stretch this to be as amazing as it could possibly be. No limits.

Love + Romance	
Career / Mission / Purpose / Impact	
Finances	
Spiritual Connection	

Friendships	
Family Relationships	
Health	
Travel	
Fun	

Living / Housing	
Quality of Life	
Accomplishments	

You can read this script out loud often or just read it, whatever works for you, but the more energy you put into it, the more likely it is to manifest in your reality. Ideally, you can print these scripts out and leave them on your nightstand, reading it every morning when you wake up, or every night before you go to bed.

I write my scripts on a Google Doc and save it onto my Google Drive. Once in a blue moon, I'll go back and review the older scripts and it is amazingly fun to see what all has come to fruition when I write from joy and no expectation.

ENERGY HEALING: FILLING UP THE THROAT CHAKRA

Our Throat Chakra is a vital area to bridge what we desire in our hearts and bring it to life through our authentic expression. A balanced throat chakra helps us to powerfully speak our inner truth and live life from an aligned space so that we can thrive in our relationships, work lives and even in order to create what we desire through our manifestations. When you feel like you're a bit off balance in this area, try on some of these tools to bring you back into balance.

Visualization:

Take a few minutes to slow down and breathe deeply, until you feel a sense of stillness and peace. Close your eyes and imagine a radiant white sparkling light pouring into the top of your head, your Crown Chakra. See this light slowly travel down through your forehead, your cheekbones, over your neck and into your throat area. Imagine a dark blue spiral inside your throat appearing. As this spiral moves, notice that it is moving all of the energy within this area with a dynamic like wind, allowing areas that may have been blocked to move once again and any "dust" or stuck energy to be freed.

Focus on your breathing for a few moments. Imagine that with each inhale, you are pulling the white light energy down into the spiral to amplify the healing process. With each exhale, you are blowing out the dust and old energy that's ready to be released. Breathe deeply for a few moments and experience the white and sapphire light healing your Throat Chakra and pouring throughout the rest of your body.

Physical Tools and Support:

- Singing, toning and chanting is a wonderful way to support clearing your throat chakra.
- Take note of the music you are listening to or singing - and make sure they are words you want to be using to manifest! This can be so unconscious and we can be manifesting things we actually do not want to feel.
- Have a conversation with someone that you have been avoiding. Holding onto these kinds of energies creates major stagnancy in our energy field.
- Practice using your voice with more authenticity and honesty on a daily basis. Stretch yourself!
- Notice when you speak from a space of gossip and stop yourself.
- Read your affirmations out loud, using your voice to cement them into your reality.
- Write out your scripts to support the creation of what you desire.

Throat Chakra Affirmations:

- I speak my feelings honestly and lovingly.
- I use my voice authentically.
- It is safe to express my true needs.
- I communicate how I feel authentically and compassionately.
- I express myself with clarity and confidence.
- I use my voice to speak gratitude and love into my life.
- I am an important voice in the world and my voice is heard.
- I communicate my highest truths.

Throat Chakra Crystals:

Any blue crystal will help to support you in clearing your throat chakra. I recommend purchasing these in necklace form, so that the energy can sit on the area all day, or even just place the crystal on your throat while laying down. You can also place these crystals in your pillow while you sleep, so that the energy can absorb into you all night!

- Blue Apatite is great for public speaking and group communication.
- Lapis Lazuli helps to promote great communication and all things mental health.
- Amazonite helps to restore emotional balance.
- Kyanite supports you in speaking your truth.

Throat Chakra Essential Oils:

I will usually opt to place these oils in my hands, rub them together and breathe it in, or diffuse the oil, rather than put them on my throat as it can absorb into your throat (and sometimes that doesn't feel so good)!

- Peppermint oil helps to encourage authentic self-expression.
- Lavender oil can help calm and soothe your nerves when communicating.
- Clary sage can help balance hormones and support the thyroid.
- Geranium is said to calm down sore throats.
- Doterra has a blend called OnGuard that is an immunity booster which supports throat health.

Third Eye Chakra

Ājñā

Third Eye Chakra

Third Eye ———

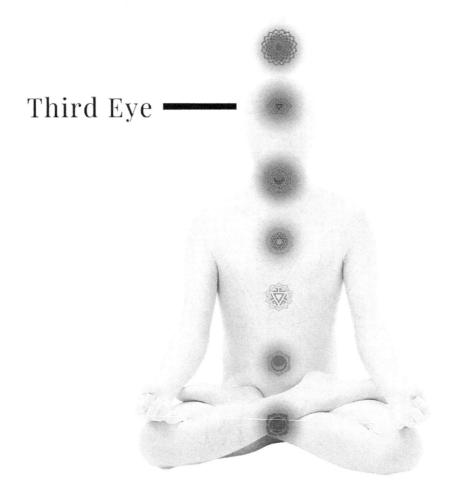

THIRD EYE CHAKRA: AJNA

Our Third Eye Chakra is a powerful chakra that helps open us up to connecting with our intuition and inner wisdom on a deeper level as well as expanding our perspective to receive guidance from higher realms. Physically, it's located between our eyebrows and is also known as our Pineal Gland, typically shown using the color indigo. As we open our third eye, we often experience a spiritual awakening. We start to see the illusions that we've been believing and that ultimately, we are the creators of our life based on how we choose to see the world and our experiences. We start to learn the power we hold as creators of our realities. As we open this chakra, we are able to "see life with new eyes."

This is the space we can manifest with ease from; where we get to take our thoughts to the next level to manifest what we'd like to create by seeing it first. This means we have to make sure we are using our energy wisely so we're manifesting what we desire! We can use our imagination to create a lot of outcomes, so we want to make sure we're using that magic power as efficiently as possible.

An imbalance in our Third Eye Chakra can look like:

- Lack of clarity
- Difficulty concentrating
- Inability to experience our intuition
- Frequent migraines
- Dizziness and fogginess
- Nightmares

In this section, we'll discuss how you can activate your third eye chakra so you can attract more of what you desire, purely through your energetic field, as well as some of my favorite tools to support you in doing so!

Don't underestimate the power of your intuition.

#SacredWealth

ABUNDANCE PRINCIPLE 32: ALWAYS TRUST YOUR INTUITION

We have a powerful sixth sense that is highly disregarded in our society: our intuition. Our intuitive sense is that inner knowing that feels like it "comes out of nowhere." We trust our intuition when it makes sense or when we have tangible evidence that supports it. For the most part, when our intuition throws us something wild, we think it is our imagination and don't pay attention to it. However, the more we listen to our intuition, the more we realize that this deep inner knowing is usually the exact guidance we need in that moment.

You've experienced your intuition so many times in your life. It might sound something like this:

- "I don't know why, but I just have a good feeling about this."
- "I can't explain why, but I feel like something is really off with him."
- "It feels like something is wrong."
- "Go to the doctor. I just have a feeling."
- "I cancelled my flight. I had a dream that something bad happened that I can't shake."
- "Something is telling me to go a different way to work today."

Our intuition speaks to us all the time! This isn't about "finding your intuition" - it's about learning how to tap into it on a more conscious basis so that you can use it to help you in your life. Your intuition can support you in all elements of your life and specifically regarding your abundance, it can help lead you to new opportunities of creating and attracting money as well as calling in more abundance with more ease.

What has your experience been with your intuition growing up?

Have you experienced intuitive nudges before? How do they show up for you?

Tuning Into Your Intuition

The first step to hearing your intuition is setting the intention to connect on a deeper level with it. Tune in with yourself and ask for help! It can be as simple as saying "I'd like to start connecting more to my intuition" to yourself.

After that, we practice getting quiet so that we can first observe our noisy thoughts that are covering up our quiet, intuitive nudges! These noisy thoughts are usually from our ego - these are the judgmental thoughts, the thoughts of comparison, the "should" thoughts. Our intuition, on the other hand, is peaceful and calm. It whispers. It is not going to raise its voice to be heard over the noisy thoughts. The only way to truly be able to hear your intuition and tap in on a deeper level is to practice stillness on a daily basis.

In the Solar Plexus section we talked about a few ways that we can practice getting still, as stillness is the fastest way to identify your thought patterns quickly. From this space, you can dentify what the most common thoughts you have are and choose if you want to keep them!

Ask yourself these questions to audit your thoughts:
1. Is this thought useful?
2. Is this thought supporting me or hurting me?
3. Is there a purpose to this thought?
4. How repetitive is this? How often does it come up during my days?

As we audit our thoughts, we clear a lot of space so that our intuition has more room to get a word in and you can hear her more easily! Once we've created more space to notice our quieter thoughts, we start to *acknowledge our subtle nudges* and how they show up for us. Everyone's intuition speaks differently, so start to pay attention to how these nudges show up for you. These may come to you through a thought, a feeling, a sensation, an inner knowing, a vision or all of the above.

How does your intuition typically show up for you? How does she nudge you?

Lastly, we have to start trusting this voice enough to listen to it and follow its guidance. The more often we take action on what our intuition tells us, the more access we will have to it. Often, we want to have tangible evidence that will "prove" the reliability of our intuition in order to follow it- but it will never happen because our intuition isn't based on reason or rationale. It's the voice of our Soul - our inner knowing. This is about starting to trust in our internal guidance. Start small!

Can you think of any gut feelings you've had in the past that guided big decisions? How did that turn out for you?

Can you think of any intuitive hits that came to you in the past that you ignored? What happened?

Has your intuition been telling you anything recently that you haven't yet taken action on?

When we listen to our intuition and act on it, it can help lead us to creating and attracting abundance with much more ease!

"Worry is a
misuse of the
imagination."

DAN ZADRA

#SacredWealth

ABUNDANCE PRINCIPLE 33: USE YOUR IMAGINATION EFFECTIVELY

Our Third Eye Chakra helps us imagine things into creation. Many of us are using our imaginations quite often without even realizing it - we must ensure that we are imagining what we desire! Have you considered that when you are worrying, you are using your imagination? The problem is, you're using your imagination and sending messages to the universe of what you do not want to happen.

"What if I can't pay my bills?"
"What if my plane is delayed and then I miss my connecting flight?"
"What if I get hurt?"
"What if it doesn't work out the way I want?"

Our fear is here to support us - if we make sure it's in check. However, most of us are checking in on it way too often and allowing worry to take over our thoughts. When we do that, we're using these recurring thoughts to imagine the worst case scenario. The Universe then sees that image and works on creating it for us, because she wants to help! She thinks that we understand all of the Universal Laws, but unfortunately we aren't taught that in school. If we think about that worry and then have the audacity to voice it, it only gains more power and momentum in being created.

What are the things you worry about most often in life?

```


```

What do you worry about most regarding money?

```


```

You might be asking, well, how can I just turn the worry off? **Face the truth that worrying is a complete misuse of your precious time.** Tune into your safety and then let it go.

> We have to realize that our time is so incredibly valuable that we can't waste it on something as silly and useless as worrying.

For example, if I purchase a plane ticket and there are connecting flights, I make sure I have a certain amount of time in between the flights so I am more likely not to miss that connecting flight. I do my due diligence by making sure I have at least 60 minutes between my flights, but that's really all I have control over. If I am on the first plane and we are delayed, sitting there worrying for the whole flight really isn't going to make an impact. If I am on the first plane and we get delayed, I will instead tell myself "This must be happening for a reason. Hopefully I make my next flight" and try to drop it. Imagining myself running to the next plane doesn't help when I don't know that is going to happen.

Additionally, having a firm belief that the Universe is always working for you will help bring you comfort, even if you are inconvenienced! I have trained myself so much in this belief that if a plane is delayed I will literally think "oh, maybe the next plane would have blown up or there would have been a major issue. I trust you, Universe. Thanks for taking care of me."

> It makes life a lot more enjoyable and less stressful when you have a baseline belief that the Universe is always taking care of you.

Parents often worry about their children. Part of this is natural - but over worrying is still a waste of your time. When you send your child off to college and you know that they may be in some new environments with new kinds of people, fear and worry may naturally come up for you. However, worrying every weekend about all the possibilities that could happen is not going to help your kid in any way - quite the opposite, actually. That worry is really just giving more energy to that scenario actually happening. **Remember, the Universe is always listening.** Do what you need to do to remove as much of the worry as possible - have a conversation with your child, get them mace and a box of condoms, and drop it. Choose to visualize them in the highest vibration possible, accomplishing their dreams and being happy, instead.

Anxiety is another area where we can misuse our imagination. Start becoming aware of the thoughts you think while you're anxious. It's normal to experience occasional anxiety, but when those thoughts start to become repetitive, we have to check in and remember -

> Wait, what directions am I giving the Universe right now?

Use Visualization as a Supportive Tool of Your Imagination

Learning how to visualize consciously will help you manifest what you desire with so much more ease. We are always attracting where we are vibrationally. So, if you are finding yourself saying "I want this, I want that" - all the Universe hears is "I don't have that" and it will keep delivering.

When we step into visualizing, we shift our reality from "wanting" something to the vibration of already having it. When we are in the process of visualization, we are telling the Universe "Thank you for this thing I already have! I am so grateful!" Basically, we are putting ourselves in the vibration of what we want, and from that space, we attract what we desire when we are vibrating there on a consistent basis.

This is proven scientifically to work, it's not just airy fairy BS. You can literally prove this - research shows that the way our neurons fire in our brains, there is very little difference between a powerful visualization and having the real experience. This is why you'll hear highly successful people and athletes talk about visualization as their secret to success. You may have heard that athletes tend to visualize before games, or even while they are injured and can't practice as much. They do this because they want to plant the seed in their subconscious mind of how the game goes and how they perform.

Many people think visualizing is hard - it's not! We just aren't practiced in it, that's all. Let's take a moment to practice. Think of this as a fun skill to learn - there's no pressure and it can look whatever way you like! There's no right or wrong way to do this, as long as you're enjoying it!

Take a moment right now to imagine a big ice cream sundae. I bet you can picture that perfectly. Are there cherries on top? Whipped cream? What flavor is the ice cream? Is the brownie underneath hot or room temperature? Does it have nuts? Chocolate or rainbow sprinkles? What color is the bowl it's in? How many spoons are in the bowl? Congratulations, you just won at visualization.

The basic steps to visualizing are to :

1. Think about the basic scenario you're imagining.
2. Start broad and then make the image more specific and clear by adding in details.
3. Allow yourself to feel the feelings you'll feel associated with what you're thinking about. Pretend you are really there in the moment.

You can visualize literally anything. Just like our intuition, we all visualize differently, so don't judge how you visualize. You may find yourself smelling that brownie sundae more than you see it in a physical image. Don't "TRY" - just let your visualization occur however it wants to happen. When you remove the pressure, you'll find that your imagination will fill in the blanks! Let the process be effortless. You literally cannot mess it up!

Visualizing is especially powerful right before you go to sleep or when you've just woken up as the body is deeply relaxed during those times and less resistant.

Here's a few examples that may help you when you're visualizing:

- New Job:
    - Imagine how you feel when you walk into work
    - What are your co-workers like?
    - How do you dress at work?
    - What's the environment like at your desk and at the building?
    - What perks do they offer you?
    - What's the work culture like?
    - How much are you getting paid and how often? See the money coming into your bank account!

- Health + Body
    - Picture yourself as radiant and gorgeous as possible - what do you look like?
    - What kind of clothes are you wearing? How do you feel in them?
    - How do you feel? What words would you use to describe it?
    - How do other people describe what you look like?
    - What's your energy level like?
    - What physical activities do you love doing?
    - What foods do you love most?
    - How do you feel about yourself when you look in the mirror naked?

- Relationships:
    - See yourself in your relationships feeling happy and fulfilled (and whatever else comes to mind that you're wanting to attract)
    - What are you doing to spend quality time in these relationships?
    - What kind of photos do you take with the people in your life?
    - What experiences are you having together?
    - How much fun are you having?
    - What do these relationships look like to someone outside looking in? How would they describe it?
    - Imagine yourself in a harmonious relationship with the people in mind and enjoying each other's company!

- Travel + Adventures:
    - Where are you traveling?
    - How do you get there? What's your transportation experience like?
    - Do you need your passport?
    - What kind of clothes did you pack in your suitcase? How big is your suitcase?
    - What kind of experiences are you having on this adventure?
    - Are you working while you're here or are you off?

Let's practice quickly with one of the areas mentioned above that you aren't attached to.

Take 3 minutes to visualize one of the areas above and write down your experience!

Did you face any resistance with visualizing? If so, what came up for you?

Great job practicing! In the next principle, we will apply this to something you're desiring to attract in your life.

"You cannot have
what you're not
willing to become
vibrationally."

MICHAEL BECKWITH

#SacredWealth

ABUNDANCE PRINCIPLE 34: MANIFEST WHAT YOU DESIRE

The concept of manifesting has blown up with popularity in the last few years, as it should! Why grind and work our tails off when we can make it easier on ourselves and enroll energetic help to support us in our goals?

With that being said, most people are missing the whole point of manifestation. When you're manifesting, the first thing that needs to be addressed is the core belief of trusting the Universe.

1. Do you trust that the Universe already has a divine plan for you?
2. Do you trust that Spirit wants the best for you?
3. Do you trust that God can create a far better result than you could ever even imagine?

We have to realize that our plans are teeny tiny compared to what the Universe has concocted for us. Most people get super attached to what they want to manifest, and that's why it never comes.

It's like if you plant a seed and then every single day you stand over it, continuing to water it, when it's already been watered too much and you drown it. It can never sprout from the ground.

What we want to do is to plant so many seeds that we aren't attached to any of them growing and sprouting. We know that the aligned ones will sprout in the perfect timing and that we'll get some amazing and miraculous surprises along the way - maybe two seeds will merge together and create a surprise plant that blows our mind! We can't be so attached to what happens after we plant the seed. We can go back and water them occasionally with love and patience, but we don't want to hover over them. Let them grow at their own pace.

Here are my 3 steps to manifesting that have supported me in attracting so much of what I desire with ease. People always tell me "it seems like you always get what you want" - well, that's because I know how to manifest and I plant so many seeds that something is always sprouting!

Aly's 3 Steps to Manifesting:

1. Get clear on what you desire.
2. Visualize the desire and get into the vibration of the desire.
3. Choose to let it go and sprout on it's own, or choose to nonchalantly focus on the desire if you can have zero attachment.

Let's get clearer on each of these steps.

Step 1: Get clear on what you desire.

Choose what you'd like to manifest, but make sure it's something you truly desire. Don't waste your time manifesting things that just feel "ok" to you. The more excited you can get about something (without attachment to it), the more momentum you are putting behind it!

I always check in with if this is a "soul goal" or an "ego goal." Sometimes we set goals because we are so conditioned that we actually really think we want something, but when we tune in, we realize our soul literally does not care about creating it. When our souls are on board with something we want to manifest, it will come with so much more ease!

> Is this a Soul Goal or an Ego Goal?

For example, most goals relating to what my body physically looks like are "ego goals" for me. My soul does not care at all what I look like - she only cares how I feel. So it's easier for me to manifest feeling healthy, vibrant, radiant and sexy rather than trying to manifest fitting in a certain outfit or looking a certain way. My soul just isn't going to get on board with having a six pack, because she doesn't care about that.

I'll ask myself two questions to see what kind of goal it is:

1. If this never happened in my life, how would I feel?
    - Soul goals - you will feel devastated, like you missed something huge. Regret.
    - Ego goals - you'll feel embarrassed or not good enough.
2. Does it matter when this happens?
    - Soul goals - you won't care as long as it happens at some point.
    - Ego goals - you'll probably set a random deadline that you care about for vanity.

Once you've got your Soul goal down, move on to the next step.

Step 2: Visualize the desire and get into the vibration of the desire.

Now we want to mimic the vibration of the thing that you desire.

1. How are you going to feel when you create this?
2. What are you going to do?
3. Who are you going to tell first?
4. How do you celebrate the win?
5. What will shift in your life when you create it?

6. What are you wearing when you see this happening?
7. What environment are you in?
8. What are the things you are saying to yourself and to others?

This is how you get into the present moment of already having it. The more you can do this, the faster it will come to you. We don't do these activities so they come quickly - we do it because being in the vibration of having it feels good and will bring it to us quicker . If your true focus is so that it will come quickly and that's in the back of your head, it will counteract the work. Just focus on visualizing because it's fun.

Step 3: Choose to let it go and sprout on it's own, or choose to nonchalantly focus on the desire if you can have zero attachment.

The hardest part for most of us in the manifesting process is letting go! We must trust that it will be this or something better. The Universe has such grander plans for us - things that we could not imagine if we expanded our brains all the way. There are so many intricate details being worked out for us behind the scenes - that we know it will be this or something better, always.

If you catch yourself asking "when is it coming" or "how much longer will it take," you have broken the manifestation gold. It won't come to you in that mindset. Patience is key with manifesting. Remember, we want to water the seeds occasionally through visualization and feeling excited with no attachment. We don't want to smother the seed asking "are you here yet?" When we're attached, it means we aren't trusting. It's that easy! We overcomplicate it.

So, I want you to think about 3 things you'd like to manifest... List them below.

1.
2.
3.

Now, take each of those manifestations and let's break them down.

1. What will it feel like when you create this?
2. Who will you tell about it?
3. Who will be there next to you?
4. What kind of clothes are you wearing?
5. What environment are you in?
6. How do you celebrate?
7. What are you doing?

Take 3 minutes minimum to visualize each desire you'd like to manifest and write down what comes up for you below! Use the questions and prompts above to help you if you get stuck. Remember, the whole point is just to have fun and let yourself play with your imagination! It doesn't need to look a certain way.

1.

2.

Tools to Support You In Manifesting With Ease

We don't need a bunch of fancy tools and tricks to manifest - we just need the 3 steps that we just discussed. However, making it more fun never hurts! Here are a few of my favorite tips and tricks to bring some fun and extra power to manifesting work:

Vision Boards

Vision boards are collections of photos that you can look at to inspire you to become the vibrational match of that which you desire. These are one of the most well-known tools that we have for manifesting. Vision boards can be physically represented on posters, on your wall, on your refrigerator, your desktop wallpaper, your phone's background or even Pinterest boards or Instagram Saved Boards. Typically people will get a bunch of magazines, cut out pictures that inspire them and glue them onto a posterboard that they put on their wall. Making vision boards is so fun - I'd encourage you to make one if you haven't before, or if yours needs a refresh!

There are a few special tricks I do differently with vision boards:

1. Stop using magazines for your photos! They aren't specific enough. Use the internet to search for the photos that exactly represent what you're looking for. Pinterest is a great place to search!

2. Make sure your photos make you feel happy and excited. Don't put a picture of a girl who looks like you, except she weighs 20 pounds less, so that when you look at her you're like "Well, still don't look like that!" You will never manifest anything that way, it's just going to make you feel bad about yourself. Not needed, or nice. Maybe a certain workout outfit would inspire you more to lose those 10 pounds and when you look at that photo, it gets you more excited to go for a run. **Make sure the pictures raise your vibration and inspire you.**

3. When you are making your vision board, write the date on the back of the photo before you tape it onto your poster board. When the thing manifests, take the photo off of your poster, write the date that it manifested on the back, and add it into a "Manifestation Magic Box." It is seriously fun to look through the box of all the things you've manifested and flip over your images to see how quickly you manifested them. My box is big now and some things take years to manifest while others happen in 2 days. This helps to remind me that everything will manifest in it's Divine timing.

I have been loving using Instagram's saved boards as a way to create vision boards. There's so much visual beauty on Instagram - I have over 20 boards now that I've created for areas like "Travel Board", "Divine Counterpart", "Dreamy Houses", "Soul Mission", "Golden Retrievers", "Mood", "Bali", etc. You can use Pinterest in the same way!

I'd also recommend keeping a folder on your computer or on Google Drive called "Vision Boards" and taking a photo of all the vision boards you make so that over the years, you can go back and look at them and see how your goals and priorities change over time.

Magic Checks

Magic checks are such a fun tool to play with! Google "Magic Checks The Secret" or look on www.thesecret.tv and you'll find a bunch that you can print out. I've also included this in the Book Resources list at www.AlyWilkins.Me. Basically, it's like the Universe is writing you a check and you use that to attract a certain amount of money to you by a certain date. I don't *love* the deadline of the dates, but if you can remain unattached to the date, it is just a fun tool to attract certain amounts of money into your life! Everytime you look at this check, feel the gratitude of that money being in your bank account and use it as a visualization tool that you can see everyday prominently.

The Magic Check — THE GRATITUDE BANK OF THE UNIVERSE. DATE _____. REMITTANCE ADVICE – Gratitude. PAY _____. TO THE ORDER OF _____. NOT NEGOTIABLE. DRAWER: THE GRATITUDE BANK OF THE UNIVERSE, ACCOUNT: UNLIMITED ABUNDANCE. SIGNED: The Universe. This is not an instrument subject to Article 3 of the UCC. |: 843 62442 |: 843 732738 843. www.thesecret.tv

Crystal Magic

Ok, crystals are magical and each kind of crystal holds its own specific energy. You can also set your own intentions to add into crystals as well so they hold a special charge.

I use crystals in so many ways - I have spent a great amount of time educating myself about the energy behind all of the crystals I have and in the morning, I'll choose my crystal jewelry based on my intention for the day. For example, right now I'm wearing several grounding bracelets so that I can remain focused in writing this portion of the book! Now there are so many ways to educate yourself - there are crystal books you can buy or a quick google search "crystals for anxiety" and you'll find many options. I also recommend going to your local metaphysical shop and just asking the people who work there for their suggestions for whatever you would like support with. Trust if you are drawn to a certain crystal, whether you are buying online or in person. I always try to buy in person, when possible, so you can sense the energy of the shop or person selling it. There are different grades and quality levels of crystals and unfortunately, some people do sell fakes, so it's best if you can feel out someone's energy.

I also use crystals for my personal and spiritual growth and healing. When I first started working with crystals, most of my work at the time was in clearing my sacral chakra, so I had carnelian stones everywhere. I wore bracelets, had a big raw chunk of carnelian by my bed, slept with small chunks in my pillowcase, brought them to work, put one in my pocket or in my bra, and even kept some in my car. I know, extreme. But, I did a lot of healing in that area and it happened very quickly!

If you are a crystal newbie, here are the crystals I'd suggest for your basic crystal tool kit:

- Clear Quartz for clearing your energy
- Selenite for clearing your energy and enhancing your intuition
- Amethyst for peace, tranquility and serenity
- Citrine for optimism, positivity and abundance
- Pyrite for good luck and manifestation
- Rose Quartz for unconditional love (for self or others)
- Carnelian for energy, confidence and creativity

I have a huge amount of crystals now because I have seen how much they shift my energy. I literally don't even wear normal jewelry hardly ever anymore - it has to be crystals! When I wake up in the morning, I'll place a few crystals on my pillowcase to help cultivate the right energy in my bed while I'm away. For example, if I had a nightmare, I would put a clear quartz piece on my pillowcase to help clear that nightmare energy away. If I'm working with a lot of self-love or wanting to be nicer to myself, I might put a rose quartz crystal on my pillowcase.

Essential Oils

Essential oils are another way that you can create a shift in your energy to raise your vibration! Essential oils are plant-based essences that act as a plant medicine for the body. When you apply these topically or diffuse them, they can help to shift your mood or vibration.

If I need some grounded energy, I'll put some Cypress oil or another grounding oil on my feet and hands and notice a shift. If I'm having trouble sleeping, I'll diffuse some lavender in the room and be asleep so fast. When I am doing my Akashic Record Readings or Reiki Healing Sessions, I use Frankincense, the Holy Oil, to help connect with Spirit on a deeper level. There is literally an oil for everything!

Make sure you are buying a high quality oil - I would not buy them from most stores. I personally use DoTerra oils and have vetted their process and trust them. If you'd like to purchase their oils through me, you can go to my website www.AlyWilkins.Me or e-mail me at alywilkinsabundance@gmail.com and I'll help get you all set up. At the date I'm writing this, there are not regulations for essential oils, so unfortunately a lot of the oils on the market are basically fragrances masquerading as a natural oil. Just be discerning in the brands you buy from! If the brand doesn't show you how they source their oils, don't buy from them.

Journal Prompts for Manifestation

This is an easy tool to add onto your morning gratitudes! Our subconscious mind does not know what's real or not - it operates from our language, cues and how we feel. Write out things that you desire as if you have already manifested them. The only rule is to write it in present tense! See examples below:

---

3 Manifestations I'm Grateful For

1. **I am so thankful for the beautiful reviews this book has received. They touch my heart. I knew that what I was sharing was powerful, but I had no idea how intensely it would affect the individuals who read it. The notes I get about the impact readers have received makes my heart so happy. I'm so thankful I listened to my intuition!** See what I mean? At the time of writing this, I obviously don't have reviews for the book yet. I'm starting to plant those seeds and get into the feeling that will ultimately manifest that desire.

2. **I am so in love with the new types of retreats I am hosting abroad. I love that I get to host retreats in magical places like Bali and Egypt, and support women with getting deep into their spiritual history and magical gifts. The type of people who are attracted to these retreats are just a dream to work with. I'm so**

---

thankful. Now, in this one, I'm stating some truths so I'm definitely tricking my subconscious. I've had extremely magical women come to all of my retreats in the US and I'm always blown away at how aligned each individual is with the work we're doing at the retreats. However, I haven't had any retreats internationally yet, so I'm just planting seeds for that to continue.

3. **I feel so excited and in awe at the same time - two publishers are fighting over my book deal and each keep offering me a higher price point. I can remember writing this on a post-it note at one point and sticking it on my wall.** Visualize this with me, please haha! Feel free to imagine seeing this book at Barnes and Noble. Thank you.

Your turn! Write 3 Manifestations You're Grateful For (in Present Tense)

Know what your version of success looks and feels like.

#SacredWealth

ABUNDANCE PRINCIPLE 35: KNOW YOUR SUCCESS QUALIFIERS

It's so vital that we get clear on what success means to us in the first place. During different phases of our lives, this will likely change, but let's get clear on what success looks like for you today:

What did success for you mean to the individuals who raised you?

What does success mean to you? If you see yourself as successful, what would that look like? What would it feel like?

What does success mean to you when it comes to financial abundance?

Taking money out of it, what does success look like for you?

Why are these things important to you?

If you were absolutely guaranteed success, what would you try? What dream would you make a move on?

Who are some people that you see as being successful? What about them embodies success to you?

In the book *Think and Grow Rich*, Napoleon Hill talks about having a Board of Advisors who he consults with often. This board is made up of people who are long dead, alive or could even be fictional characters. He would meet with this group and consult them with questions about life, business, etc as if they were real right in front of him and receive mentorship from this group. After reading about this, I created a board with people I admired and assigned them each a role and title, as if this was a real life Board for my company. A few of the people on my Board:

- Beyonce :   Advisor of Work Ethic and Dreaming Impossibly Big
- Oprah: Advisor of Impact, Service and Mindset
- Tony Robbins: Advisor of Personal Growth and Financial Success
- Kris Jenner :   Advisor of Branding + Publicity
- Lakshmi: Advisor of Abundance and Prosperity
- Ganesha :   Advisor of Removing Obstacles
- Marie Forleo: Advisor of Authenticity
- Wayne Dyer: Advisor of Faith and Intuitive Wisdom

If you created such a Board to consult with for your success, who would be on it? What would their roles be?

ENERGY HEALING: FILLING UP THE THIRD EYE CHAKRA

Our Third Eye is a powerful area for truly seeing - seeing beyond the ego, beyond the illusions. When we allow it to open, we can gain a whole new kind of clarity. This is the space where we can activate so many of our spiritual gifts that most of us have not yet tapped into. Additionally, it's one of our power centers for manifestation. Use these tools when you want to sharpen your third eye's line of sight or feel more focused and clear in your life.

Visualization:

Take a few deep breaths and get rooted in your center. Bring yourself to a place of calmness and groundedness. Close your eyes and imagine a royal purple amethyst gem rotating a few inches in front of your Third Eye. See this gem slowly spinning, as if it unlocking the Third Eye. Take your time with this. It's almost like someone is wiping off a foggy camera lens - the longer the gem rotates, the clearer your sight becomes. You can feel your third eye fully opening, unlocking all of the power of your Pineal Gland. Once you've completed this exercise, give your third eye a few gentle taps to signal to it that it is safe to wake up, and say "Thank You."

Physical Tools and Support:

- Meditation and stillness will help you activate your Third Eye Chakra most deeply.
- Physically tap on your Third eye as if you are saying "time to turn on" or "let's activate deeper."
- Live with an open mind and practice exploring different perspectives.
- Ask for help. "Spirit, please help me to see this clearly. Please sharpen my sight so I'm looking from an undistorted lens of love."
- Utilize imagery and visualization to help you get clear on what you want!
- Practice candle gazing.
- When meditating with your eyes closed, practice looking upward toward your third eye.
- Detoxify your diet - drink clean water, remove processed foods, limit caffeine and other substances and eat real food (food that is natural to Earth and not made in a lab).

Third Eye Affirmations:

- I trust my intuition and follow it without question.
- I listen to my deepest wisdom.
- I am connected to my Higher Self.
- I am present.
- I am open to diving guidance.
- I have a clear vision.
- It is safe for me to trust my inner guidance.

Third Eye Chakra Crystals:

Give yourself a crystal healing and place one of these crystals over your third eye for 30 minutes while listening to high vibrational music!

- Tiger's eye for heightened intuition and clear receiving of guidance
- Amethyst for wisdom, healing and access to your Higher Self
- Lapis Lazuli for awareness, intuitive sharpness and mental health
- Purple fluorite for heightened intuition

Third Eye Chakra Essential Oils:

You can place these oils directly on your third eye with a carrier oil, diffuse them or breathe them in by rubbing the oil between your hands.

- My Favorite: Frankincense , the Holy Oil, for access to higher realms
- Lavender for centered and calm energy
- Clary Sage for balancing emotions and seeing clearly
- Rosemary for gentle opening
- Sandalwood for self-reflection and knowledge

Crown Chakra

Sahasrāra

Crown Chakra

Crown ———

CROWN CHAKRA: SAHASRARA

The Crown Chakra is our highest Chakra wheel in our physical body and helps to connect us with our Higher Self. This area represents wisdom, presence, awareness, peace, enlightenment and universal consciousness - the feeling and knowing of oneness. It's the meeting point of the Divine and our Physical Self. Physically, the Crown Chakra is located at the top of our head. You'll see this area represented by the colors violet or white.

The Crown Chakra is the place where we transcend our ego - and identify not as a human in a physical body, but as a soul living in a body. When this area is open, we can have a meaningful connection with the Divine. This is where our spiritual connection enters the body, so when it is blocked, we may feel disconnected from Spirit. On the other hand, we can also feel so attached to Spirit that we have a hard time feeling grounded in our bodies (think of this as living in the clouds, unable to focus or get anything physical done).

To me, this is the area where all the fun begins as we get to really play in the Spiritual world and open up to what truly abundant living looks like, according to us! Please keep an open mind as I take you through my experience of what has supported me in feeling abundant. Take or leave what you like and trust what you are drawn to!

Understand that you're never alone. You have an enormous cosmic support team who is constantly cheering you on.

#SacredWealth

ABUNDANCE PRACTICE 36: WORK WITH YOUR COSMIC SUPPORT TEAM

A few years ago, I started saying that I had a cosmic support team. I hadn't heard anyone use this term before, but it kept popping in my head. Back then, I was new to the world of angels, spirit guides, ancestral guidance, animal totems, etc. Now that I operate and work in this space in many ways, I know that the feeling of having a huge team of support in other realms was completely accurate.

Sometimes, it can feel like we are alone here on Earth, but the truth is that we have a whole squad of cheerleaders standing behind us at all times who are silently giving us guidance and support throughout our journey. You may not see them, but they are there and are available for support and guidance at any time.

In my retreats, we often have group ceremonies where we call in a few members of our support team. We create incredibly sacred ceremony, setting our intentions and then going on a journey together with Cacao, the Akashic Records and intentional music. During this journey, we dive into the heart space and as the women go in deeper, their guides start to appear and make contact. This may just feel like chills, visions or feeling touch on various parts of the body, but at a certain point the entire room will be full of all of our guides, trying to squeeze in to give as much support as possible. I see the women's individual guides standing behind them, placing comforting hands on shoulders, reminding that all is well and that they are *so beyond proud of you*. Usually these ceremonies are highly emotional because it is so easy to feel alone in our world today, but there is nothing further from the truth. Know that you are supported and whether you can see or feel it or not, you have someone with you right now as you read this. They likely were the ones who led you to this book.

Take a moment to experience this for yourself. Slow down. Take several deep breaths and close your eyes. Imagine feeling two warm hands on your shoulders and hearing "You cannot even come close to understanding how proud we are of you. You have been moving beyond our highest timelines for you. We know the journey you've been on and are here for you every step of the way. Ask us for help. That's what we're here for. Lean on us. We love you more than you could ever imagine."

As you read that, if you really tuned in (and didn't just skim it), what did you feel?

Have you ever had signs appear to you that seem just too coincidental? Have you ever had synchronicities occur that you cannot explain? This is the work of your Cosmic Support Team. They won't take credit or say "I told you so," but they're always watching and guiding you. They don't judge when you mess up (again), they just scoot the tissue box a centimeter closer so you can reach it from bed and deliver signs to you that they hope you'll catch.

I'll give you a quick overview of some of the types of guides who are on your support team - so you can be aware of them and learn how to ask them for support. Tune into what you feel guided towards here as there is a plethora of information you can learn about each of these groups.

Spirit Guides

I believe that your spirit guides are made up of a variety of entities - Gods and Goddesses, your Higher Self, Ancestors, Angels, Animal Spirits and more. All of these spirits make up your team of Spirit Guides. Let's break them down a little more here:

Angels

Angels are one of my favorite groups of guides to work with because they feel so incredibly safe and loving. Angels represent unconditional love and can be reached in a moment's notice - we only have to ask. You have a few angels who are "assigned" to you from birth, but you can call upon any angel at any time to help you with specific challenges or tasks.

The archangels are a powerful group of angels that you can call upon - they are the "chiefs" of the angels, if you will. There are many archangels that you can learn about if you so feel called, but these are the five who have appeared most in my readings and in my personal work that feel most powerful (and available) to me:

- Archangel Michael
  - Offers physical and spiritual protection
  - Works very closely with Lightworkers

- Archangel Gabriel
  - Supports Divine Communication
  - Works with mothers and children
  - Supportive for inner child work

- Archangel Raphael
  - Supports physical, mental and emotional Healing
  - Provides emotional comfort

- Archangel Jophiel
  - Supports you with Divine Beauty
  - Shifts negativity into positivity

- Archangel Zadkiel
  - Supports Divine Forgiveness
  - Helps to transmute negativity back into light

Animal Totems

Animals are an important part of your support team as well. Pay attention to the animals that show up in your life. I'm not talking about the dog who lives next door - he literally lives there. I'm talking about the random red bird that shows up on your windowsill when you're contemplating what to do. I'm talking about the caterpillar who crawls over your foot. I'm talking about the flurry of butterflies that flies past you when you say "just show me a sign!"

You may feel drawn to certain animals and have since you were a child. Typically, we have a few power animals who guide our journeys and those animals will hold important guidance for us through our path. There will also be different animals that pop up for specific lessons that you require support with. Just become aware - animals are souls as well and they bring us important messages!

Ancestors

Some of the people in your lineage who have passed on are available for you to connect with. You can reach them at a moment's notice, if they are available to you (not all of them want to be reached or are at the vibration that they are healthy to do so). These guides will have valuable information for you regarding your own lineage and family healing that can take place. It is especially sentimental if you had the chance to know some of these people in your physical lifetime because you'll be able to recognize certain elements when you meet them - their demeanor, their smell, how they appear, their personality, etc. For example, the other day, I was doing an Akashic Record reading and said "I'm seeing a woman sitting on this purple velvet couch, smoking a cigarette with a bold and eccentric attitude - she does what she wants and is extremely blunt." My client instantly said "oh, yes that sounds just like my grandmother who passed away 10 years ago."

Gods and Goddesses

Different Gods and Goddesses from many cultures may appear during certain parts of your life to support you. For example, I work very closely with Ganesha, Remover of Obstacles, and Lakshmi, Goddess of Abundance, on a daily basis to help me remove obstacles in my life and attract abundance. I love working with them so much, I created a 40 Day Sacred Wealth Ritual that utilizes their support to attract abundance to you - you can purchase that on my website, if you'd like a committed practice that can help you call in more abundance while utilizing the powers of these powerful deities! Recently, I've been guided to working with Mary Magdalene, Ra, Isis, Sekhmet and Anubis and I look forward to seeing their impact in my life. If you grew up going to church often, you may already have certain Saints or similar figures that you feel very connected to. Trust who finds you - that's all I'm going to say!

Plant Elementals

This may be a little "out there" for you, but plants also have intense healing abilities. If you try to communicate with a plant, you will get a response (if you are open and receptive to it). Notice that when you communicate with your flowers, they seem to grow healthier. You can experience the unconditional love that plants have to offer while they are living and also experience their intense healing capabilities (safely) through a shaman or another practitioner that you trust when they are in other forms.

It is my suggestion to try to use plants as often as possible instead of pharmaceuticals. Most pharmaceuticals are mimicking the power of plants, just cost a lot more and have a lot more chemicals and side effects. Do not do this without a doctor's help if you are on medication, just find a doctor who won't laugh at you when you ask them about this! Unfortunately, most doctors who study western medicine don't believe in the power of holistic healing, even though it's what was done for thousands of years prior to western medicine across the globe. Pharmaceuticals are a blessing in many ways to help us with serious conditions; however, like a naturopath, I believe we get to try using nature's medicines as a first route, whenever possible.

Akashic Records

I've spoken a bit about the Akashic Records, because it's one of my favorite modalities of healing. Imagine a big library, full of lots of books. Each book contains the history and future of an individual soul. There are guardians who protect these books so someone cannot come in and flip through all the pages of your book. They also don't want YOU to do this either! As humans, we get too attached and make meaning out of things that don't always matter. So, when I take someone into the Akashic Records as their guide and channeler, the Guardian of the Records will send over the appropriate guides from your cosmic support team to share the messages that will support you in this moment. I just share the information that they give me. A wide variety of experiences can occur in your journey in the Akashic Records - you could connect with ancestors, spirit guides, animal totems, angels, past lives, etc. It is an incredible tool to utilize in your healing journey! Reach out to me if you'd like to book a session at AlyWilkinsAbundance@gmail.com.

Have you ever felt connected to a spirit that you couldn't see? Do any of these kinds of support feel familiar to you?

Are there any Gods, Goddesses, Saints, etc that you feel a connection to?

How do you feel about spirit guides in general? Resistant? Excited? Unsure? (However you feel is perfect!)

Do you feel drawn to connect further with your Spirit Guides or learn more about any of the kinds of support that we mentioned above?

Your energy is your most important and precious asset that you have.

#SacredWealth

ABUNDANCE PRACTICE 37: MASTER ENERGETIC PROTECTION

While there are many ways you can protect yourself that we talked about in the Solar Plexus Chakra section, this topic is going to support you with energetically protecting yourself, especially as you go deeper into your spiritual awakening.

A few tools that will support you in clearing energy :

- Sage bundles are dried sage leaves that you can burn to completely clear all energy. This is something you'd want to use if you have a big argument, you're moving into a new home and you want to clear the energy completely, or you want a fresh new vibe.
- Palo Santo is a kind of tree that you can burn to remove all negative energy from your space. The positive energy will remain.
- Crystals, of course, particularly clear quartz and selenite. To keep the energy of a space clear and protected, you can put a crystal in each of the four corners of the room, ideally a protective crystal or clearing crystal.
- Particular essential oil blends that you can diffuse that support with clearing the space - typically you'll find these made with citrus oils.
- Epsom salt helps to detoxify your system and clear energy. Add a few cups to a very hot bath and soak for 20-30 minutes. Allow the tub to drain before you get out, so that the toxins are "sucked" out of your skin and then rinse off in the shower after (to rinse the remaining toxins off your skin). Bentonite clay can also support with detox as well.
- You can even ring a bell to clear energy!

Grounding Your Energy

As you work in the higher realms and explore your spiritual process, it's important to stay grounded. It's easy to fly off into the ethers and start to feel like you can't focus or get anything done. Getting grounded again will support you. In addition, if you ever feel anxious or stressed, grounding will help you come back to a place of calm and centeredness. We briefly discussed this at the end of the Root Chakra section, but I'll include it again here as well, as it is that important!

A few of my favorite ways to ground my energy:
- Put your bare feet in the grass, sand or soil to absorb Mother Earth's energy.
- Spend as much time in nature as possible.
- Stomp your feet, ideally on the ground level or in nature.
- Visualize yourself in nature, ideally sitting in grass, sand or soil, if you are not able to physically go out in nature.
- Physically wipe energy off of your body   *dirt off your shoulder* as well as your lower back, sides of your torso and anywhere else you feel you're holding energy.

- Eating is also a grounding activity! It helps "weigh you down" and bring you back into your body.
- Listen to the beating of a drum, or play your drum if you have one.
- Practice breathwork to bring you back into your body.
- Hold crystals that help you connect to Earth energy, like Red Jasper, Bloodstone, Kamababa Jasper, Galena, Hematite or Leopard Skin Jasper.

Place Yourself in an Energy Bubble of Protection

When you are physically going out, you can always utilize an energy bubble! Gabby Bernstein calls this "The Zip Up." Imagine yourself in a big onesie and you bend over to zip it up from the bottom of your feet, all the way up your body, and then allow the zipper to continue moving to the back of your body, completely zipping up through the back of your heels. You can physically move your arms along with this motion, if this supports you, or just imagine placing yourself in an energy bubble. The idea behind this is that as you encapsulate yourself in this space, no other energy is able to penetrate your auric field.

Cord Cutting Ceremony

We create energetic cords (attachments) to other people, with even small interactions. These attachments could connect anywhere to your body - if you really try to tune in, you may feel where they are. I feel the vast majority of my attachments in my torso. So imagine these attachments are ropes or strings connecting from your body to someone else's body and the weight of the connections may tug at you - they feel heavy and drain your energy. It's important occasionally to cut these cords, especially with people who are causing you problems in your relationships or have heavy energy. When you cut these cords, you're not hurting the relationship at all, you're just not holding onto their energy. It's only a way to release energy that is not yours. There are no negative implications for anyone. You can cut cords with anything, it doesn't necessarily have to be a person. You could cut cords with expectations, fears, or situations you want to release.

Archangel Michael is a wonderful support for this exercise. You can make this as casual or fancy of a ceremony as you'd like. Here's the process I go through when I cut cords:

- Think about the person or situation that you want to detach from energetically. Again, you're not harming the relationship at all, I just don't want to feel the weight of their energy. We're only supposed to carry our own energy!
- Call upon Archangel Michael and request his presence and support.
- See Archangel Michael using golden scissors to cut the attachments. For me, thicker attachments feel like big ropes and smaller attachments might be very thin rope or string. When I do a more casual version of this, I just do "air scissors" around the area I feel the attachments and know that I'm cutting the cords myself.
- Thank Archangel Michael for his support and notice how you feel.

You could do this as a daily practice, especially if you work with a lot of people daily, or whenever you feel called to. If you've just experienced a breakup, this is a great time to practice this everyday until you no longer feel your ex's energy pulling on you.

Working with Spirits

Scary movies have skewed our thinking in what connecting with the spirit world is like. They do not have extra powers or have any additional control over us. We can command them to leave us alone at any time. You create the container and set the rules. When my medium abilities started showing up, passed souls would come to me all throughout the day, which would throw me off while I was learning how to navigate these gifts. Imagine trying to get work done and you look to the right and see a line of spirits to your right. Eventually I started saying " I am not available right now. Come back tomorrow in the afternoon when I'm done with my project and I can help you then."

When I say that you're in charge, there are still precautions to take - I'm not saying to go pull out your ouija board and summon up whoever you like - there are still safety protocols here because there are a variety of vibrational energies that come along with spirits. Just because someone has passed away, doesn't mean that they are a good vibration for you to be in connection with.

If you ever feel like you've encountered a Spirit or another energy, and you feel unsure or scared about it, all you have to do is ask **"Is this energy of love and light?"** I usually instantly receive an answer in some form (for me, it is most often audible). If you feel like it's not friendly, command it to leave by saying something like "You are not welcome here, leave now."

I remember seeing things for a long time when I'd wake up in the middle of the night and would convince myself *NOTHING TO SEE HERE* and the more you do that, the more they realize you are not open for business.

Just remember, you are always in control here and you can say "go away" or "I want to connect with you" - whatever feels right for you! You want to feel comfortable and safe in order to invite spirits and other energies in.

It's easy to have faith when everything seems like it's working. Tap into your FULL- TIME Faith.

#SacredWealth

ABUNDANCE PRACTICE 38: EMBODY FULL-TIME FAITH

True abundance is experienced regardless of the circumstance you are in financially. When you can have a baseline feeling of abundance throughout any situation - you are doing something right! Abundance is having full-time faith. This kind of faith does not waver through economic crises, challenges or hard times. You always trust that something amazing is right around the corner - and you put your attention on that. Having faith is easy when everything is going your way. True faith comes in when it seems like nothing is working, or like things are falling apart.

For example: earlier today I was having a very emotional moment. I went outside for a breather and I heard something whisper, " Aly, what are you grateful for?" I rolled my eyes, like, "Can't you just let me be dramatic and emotional for a minute?" Well, it had been a full day, so I guess they had a point. So I went along with it - "well, I'm thankful that I have great vision and I can see the view of the ocean from this balcony. I'm thankful that I got such a good deal on this vacation rental for this particular time in my life, because it was really needed. I'm thankful for the greenery I can see below the balcony. I'm thankful for the animals I can see from up here. I'm really thankful for feeling the wind on my face." What do you know? Instantly felt better. Even though I technically had a lot of things "going wrong" - when I really tuned in, I was reminded how incredibly blessed I am. It's just easier for us to focus on the negative.

When times get hard, do you focus on abundance or the problem? (or both)?

Do you feel like you have Full-Time Faith? How could you strengthen your faith?

What area of your life could use the biggest boost of faith right now?

Who is someone that you could look to as a reminder of what Relentless Faith looks like?

```



```

True abundance is when we search for the silver lining, even if it's in a pool of mud. We will find that silver lining.

Here's another example that is much more intense. When I was younger, I made the mistake of driving after I had several drinks (I know, so stupid and dangerous. Trust me when I say, I was humiliated enough to learn my lesson 1000x over. I won't even drive now after having too much coffee). I could easily look back at that moment of my life with pure regret and shame, but instead, I literally tell the story and say "it's so interesting, because I had a lot of car trouble that week, which was out of the ordinary. Someone hit the back of my car a few days prior, and then the next day, I had a tire come off while I was driving on the interstate. Maybe getting this DUI (where miraculously no one was hurt) saved me from a much more dangerous situation where I could have been seriously hurt or injured. I am actually thankful this happened because I learned so much from it, and maybe it did save me from something a lot worse." Usually I actually say, "Maybe the car would have blown up or something." Just to be real.

When we can look at incredibly difficult situations and find the lesson, that is a real abundance mindset.

What is one of the most challenging situations you've been through in your life thus far?

```



```

What did it teach you? What did you learn from it?

```



```

How did you grow from that experience?

How could you shift into gratitude for having that experience?

A lot of us have trust issues. We try to control the situation to know that we will be safe. When we live from an abundant space, we have to let go. It is so hard, I know. We have to surrender to the idea that the Universe has a plan for us and that it knows what it's doing. **The Universe / God / Source / Divine knows better than us.**

"Live as if everything is rigged in your favor." - Rumi

How can you let go of control in your life? What are you trying to control so that you can secure a certain outcome?

Let go of the how. We don't have to understand how something will work out, or how to do anything. **All we have to do is surrender.**

Sometimes surrender looks like crying on the bathroom floor, feeling like we're at our rock bottom. Sometimes it looks like those dramatic scenes in movies where someone screams up into the skies with their hands up, shaking. But it can also just look like "I need help. I don't know what to do. I don't have the answers and I'm asking for support." Surrender is humble.

Surrendering is the easiest way to create the abundant life that you want. When we think we know everything, we completely limit ourselves, because in reality we know nothing.

Where in your life can you surrender right now? What could you use some support with?

Where in your life have you been pretending you have it all together, but really you could use some support?

Take this opportunity to get specific and ask your guides for help! Write your request below.

One way that I'll ask for support is asking for signs. You can get specific and say "show me an orange butterfly. If I don't see one, that's my sign, and if I do see one, that's a sign as well." I personally don't love asking for really specific examples - I trust my guides will give me the sign that works for me. However; I do ask for really obvious signs.

"Hi Spirit Team, I would like a glaringly obvious and clear sign - one that a toddler could not miss. Can you please give me a sign about what I should do about _____?"

Sometimes our sign will reveal itself as soon as we ask it, purely from noticing which sign we want to receive. Sometimes that's a sign of what we want, but not what the most helpful guidance would be. Other times, why wouldn't we follow what we desire?

For example, if you're dating someone that you really like, but they keep blowing you off, and you ask for a sign if you should stay - you might WANT a sign that you should stay because you think they are so great. But in reality, if they are blowing you off, your guides may show you a sign that has to do with self-worth or respecting yourself.

We always choose what to do with the guidance we get, but if we are asking for a sign and then do the opposite, that's just kind of rude. Luckily, our guides love us unconditionally.

If you found out you were going to die next week, would you be happy with the way you've been living your life?

#SacredWealth

ABUNDANCE PRACTICE 39: DEVOTE YOURSELF TO MISSION

Many of us are searching for our "Life Purpose" and while I definitely believe that we have a mission for why we are here on Earth, our true purpose is to follow our joy and curiosities. To try to narrow it to one would be impossible, as I feel we have many, many purposes that shift as we age and grow. However, our purposes may all link up together into a bigger umbrella purpose that encompasses our joys, passions, excitements and curiosities. I like to call this our Soul Mission. Here's a few ideas of what this could look like:

- My Soul Mission is to help create a new way of living - one where we get to find what lights us up and create a life around that.
- Someone else's Soul Mission might be to create empowering clothing items that support all processes of an ethical garment creation process.
- Someone else's mission might be to create beautiful art that inspires people.
- Another person's mission might be to raise a family who embodies unconditional love.
- Someone else's Soul Mission might be to help people feel more beautiful.

We have to be careful that we don't follow the "American Dream" (make enough money to survive and get a nice watch and appear that you are happy, but really living a monotonous and numb life) and forget our own dream. I don't know about you, but when I'm on my deathbed, I want to know that I made an impact. That I left a solid mark on the Earth. Not that I just took care of my family. That's noble and honorable - but being blunt, it's not enough for me. It's not why I'm here. There are bigger things to be accomplished at this point.

REAL TALK:

- ❖ If you don't love what you do, why are you doing it?
- ❖ If your employer doesn't respect you or your quality of life, why are you choosing to give them the majority of your time?
- ❖ If your work doesn't create a feeling of fulfillment, why are you doing it?
- ❖ If you know what makes your heart smile and how you could figure out a way to create a career out of that, why are you not doing that?

It took me years and lots of experimentation to really figure out what my Soul Mission was - and the truth is that naming it doesn't matter at all, because these missions evolve as we do. The only thing that's truly important is to look at if what you are doing feels fulfilling, fun, joyful and worthwhile to you.

It's one thing to do something temporarily while you figure out a plan to go for your mission. There's no judgment for working a job to pay the bills. The problem I have is when your personal joys and excitements go off to the wayside. When I left the "dream job" to create my own business, several people spoke to me about how they wished they left the company 20 years ago. It's easy to get stuck somewhere. Time passes quickly. Don't be the person with regrets in 20 years.

I get the real, 3D element that bills that are sitting on the table, waiting to be paid. We have to remember, when we are radiating joy and abundance, more physical abundance will flow in as well. Do you have a base belief that life is hard, or that the Universe always supports you?

It's a myth that we have to choose between loving our work and making the money we desire. We get to create both - it's just not always such a straightforward path because the honest truth is that 95% of our society isn't doing this. Most people are just doing what they are told and following the status quo, even if they hate it. We don't have a lot of examples of people creating lives based on their Soul Mission, so we have to figure out how we can pave this path on our own, much of the time. It's highly important to surround yourself with people who are doing this so that you can stay motivated and stay on the path of your Soul, not what you "think you should be doing" according to society's (low) standards.

If you don't love what you're doing right now, stop and think about what you would rather be doing. Start getting curious and experimenting with no pressure applied.

What I've found is that trying to separate work and personal life is the problem all together. When we can tie our "work" into our personal life mission, it all combines effortlessly and your "work" will no longer feel like work.

PS - this doesn't mean you have to have your own business, it could be a simple shift of changing jobs from something that you can't stand to something that brings you fulfillment. All that matters is that you feel fulfilled and are enjoying how you spend your time.

What do you daydream about? List everything that comes to mind.

What are your biggest passions in life that you're aware of right now?

What's something that excites you that you could make money doing?

What is something you would love to do but fear you don't have the skills to be successful in?

In the coaching and facilitation work I do, I talk to people all the time who know exactly what they want to do but stay at the job they hate because they are afraid. Let me be clear - pursuing your Soul Mission is not easy by any means. You will have to face so many of your survival-based fears. People won't understand what you're doing or why you're doing it. They won't understand why you would possibly leave a safe situation just to "follow your heart."

It's a new paradigm and a new age. We get to create our lives from our heart now - and honestly, thinking about living any other way is just devastating. What a waste of a precious life.

We're all gifted with such unique skills, traits and personalities and that is all on purpose. Have you ever found a book, show, video online or even just a friend at the exact perfect time? The message found you in the exact moment that you needed it? In order to hear it, you needed that personality or the way someone said something for it to really land. We think that we are just normal and average, and we are definitely "regular" - but we are unique in our gifts. We are ordinary and extraordinary at the same time.

Our dreams are incredibly unique and on purpose. We have to trust them. We have to trust that the world would be a better place when we create our dreams.

I don't know about you, but I don't feel motivated or inspired by Joe Schmo who is going along with the status quo saying things like "only 3 days left til the weekend!" However, when I see someone who has really gone for their dreams, I respect that person highly. They inspire me to be my best. That's more of what we need in this world. We don't have to get it perfectly right - we just have to go for it and tap into our Full Time Faith that it will work out exactly how it's meant to.

There are many fears that we have to move through when we choose to live from SOUL, but the biggest thing I think people should be worried about is *spending your days doing something you don't love*. How much time do you spend working? That's a lot of time to be checking the clock to see how much time you have left til you can go home for the day. That's a lot of time you're wishing and wasting away. What else could you be doing with that valuable time?

Here's a quick way to tune into if you're happy with what you're doing and how you've spent your time so far . Ask yourself this question often.

> If I died next week, would I be happy with the way I've been spending my life?

If you died next week, would you be happy with the way you've spent your life? Write whatever comes up for you here.

What are some things that you want to experience that you haven't experienced yet?

What would you want to shift? What would feel fulfilling to you?

We just have to determine what's most important to us in our life. Enjoying my time is highly important to me. Contributing to the world and using the gifts God gave me feels incredibly important to me. Sitting at a job I don't like just for a steady paycheck doesn't feel like a good use of my time. Just check in with what makes your life fulfilling and meaningful - and follow that.

What's most important to you in your life? Underneath the bills and society-driven "have to's" - what matters to you?

I have many resources on my website (www.AlyWilkins.Me) that can support you with this concept - check it out if you'd like help in this area! You can also always email me (AlyWilkinsAbundance@gmail.com) to schedule a call with me if you want 1:1 support here.

Our vibration creates our experience of life.

#SacredWealth

ABUNDANCE PRACTICE 40 : TREAT EVERYTHING AS SACRED

We can go through the motions of life and the mundane moments, skipping through them and barely even noticing - but when we treat everything as sacred, it allows us to let miracles flow in with much more ease because we are in the vibration of appreciation.

Think about this. How do you put your moisturizer on at the end of the night? Do you slap it on as fast as possible? Or do you really get present, feeling the textures of your products and showing appreciation towards your skin? Setting the intention of adding some love to your skin that brings so much beauty into your life. Do you know how many people want that moisturizer you're using? How many people think that would be *oh, so luxurious* to be able to do that? We have to remember to appreciate the small things and the small moments of life.

Creating Rituals for Anything - Add a Sprinkle of Love and Gratitude Into Everything

I create rituals out of literally everything. In the morning, I set up my crystal grids in my home. Typically I'll have a similar setup and just move a few crystals around based on the vibration I want to create for the day. I place a few crystals on my pillowcase, setting the intention to add a certain energy into the pillowcase for my sleep that night. I go through my crystal bracelets and choose the ones that will support me that day, based on the energy that they offer.

When I'm working on a project, I set the intention for what I want to cultivate and bring candles, crystals, incense and other devotional items into my space to help support me. I call upon my guides and angels to support my drive to Target and finding the right items I need, without overbuying or thinking I need more than I really do. I ask Ganesha to help remove obstacles in my life or with my career endeavors.

When I make my coffee in the morning, I imagine adding the ingredients of love, focus and ____ (insert whatever your intention is for the day) as I stir the sugar and creamer. I infuse it with Reiki energy to help me create the most healing day possible.

When I make a homemade meal, I offer gratitude to the people who grew my food, the driver who brought it to the grocery store or the farmer's market, the person who bagged my groceries, and for my clients who helped fund my ability to purchase food from someone else and contribute to the local economy. This brings a different magic to our food that we absorb as we eat it.

When I facilitate ceremonies for groups, or even conduct my own healing ceremonies, I act as if it's the most sacred act I've ever done. I clean up the area, using sage or palo santo to cleanse the space, hand select crystals to use and pull oracle cards to help guide my sessions.

Before I sat down to write this chapter, I burned sage to remove any negative energy from the space. I put my Ganesha totem in front of a beautiful candle, surrounded by dried flowers from the bouquet I received last week. As I lit the candle, I invoked the energy of Egyptian Goddess Sesheta to help remove obstacles during my writing process and to help support me with staying focused. I put on energy healing music. It's a whole vibe. The intention behind it is what makes the difference - it creates a different feeling and vibration in my space.

> When we treat something as sacred, we're going to get a lot more out of it.

I could chug my coffee before I have to run out the door,, but what does that do to my body and my state of mind, as compared to if I take a few moments to really appreciate and enjoy it, being present with the taste, warmth, texture and how it makes me feel?

How can you make your everyday moments more sacred?

What is one thing that you could ask for more support with from your Guides?

How to Create Sacred Space

To create sacred space, all you have to do is set the intention to shift the vibration. It can look however you'd like it to. You don't need any physical tools at all - only your consciousness and awareness. Here are a few words you can use to help shift the vibration of your space:

- "All negative energy will leave this space now."
- "I am creating a space of focus and presence."
- "I allow all forms of creativity and divine guidance into my space now."
- "I ask ____ for support with _____. Thank you."

Remember, our vibration creates our reality. We attract everything from our vibrational point of being. Adding intention and appreciation into your everyday activities will only raise your vibration and help you feel more radiant and abundant.

<u>ENERGY HEALING: FILLING UP THE CROWN CHAKRA</u>

The Crown Chakra is the area where our true realization of our innate oneness comes to our awareness - that we are not really individuals, but a collective. That we are unique in our creation, but are all connected and here to support one another. This is the gateway to spiritual wisdom and enlightenment. Use these tools when you'd like to activate this area.

Visualization:

Get comfortable and take a few moments of deep breathing to center yourself. Imagine yourself in a beautiful, large green field. You look in front of you and see an enormous tree. This tree seems 1,000 years old - it's so large and feels like it holds a lot of wisdom. As you glance over the leaves, you notice that there are beautiful golden orbs hanging off each branch. Imagine that one of these orbs starts to hover away from the tree and come towards you slowly. Imagine these healing golden orbs circling around you, with a single orb moving towards the top of your head, where it hovers for a moment.

You see the orb transform into a large golden pillar, connecting with the sky energy and pulling its energy down into your crown area, connecting with your third eye, your throat and your heart. Feel the tranquility and peace filling your body, absorbing every cell with this healing light. It continues to move throughout your body, swirling through your solar plexus, your sacral chakra and your root chakra. It moves gracefully down through your hips, your legs, your ankles until it reaches the heels and spreads across your feet. From this place, you can feel the light moving down into the earth from your feet. Your roots sprout from the bottom of your feet and the energy moves quickly down into the center of the earth, connecting you with Mother Earth's grounded energy. You are completely held by the groundedness of the Earth and lifted by the inspiration of the Cosmos. Bring yourself back to your seat and notice how your body feels at this moment.

Physical Tools and Support:

- Do your own color therapy healing! Each color has a different vibration and supports different elements of our healing. For crown healing, use white, purple or gold.
- Drink herbal teas like peppermint and ginger tea.
- Pray in whatever way feels aligned for you.
- Make sure you are grounded as you open your crown chakra so you don't feel like you are floating in airy fairy world!
- Akashic Record Readings are one of my favorite modalities to work with the crown chakra and gain information and guidance from your guides. I offer these sessions, as well as many others! If you'd like to book a session, visit my website www.AlyWilkins.Me or e-mail me at AlyWilkinsAbundance@gmail.com

- There are a wide variety of energy healing modalities - trust what you are called to:
  - Reiki
  - Chakra balancing
  - Acupuncture
  - Psychic healings
  - Soul retrievals
  - Past life regression

Crown Affirmations:

- I honor the Divine within.
- I am at peace.
- I am connected to the Universe.
- I see the beauty and divinity in all things.
- I feel connected to my Higher Self.
- I am attuned to the divine energy of the universe.

Crown Chakra Crystals:

- Clear Quartz for clearing energy.
- Selenite for removing blockages and creating clarity.
- Amethyst for peace, tranquility and psychic development.
- Moonstone for development of psychic awareness.
- Howlite to stabilize the emotions.

Crown Chakra Essential Oils:

You can place these oils directly on your crown,, diffuse them or breathe them in by rubbing the oil between your hands. I also place the oil on my feet and hands, as these areas are very receptive to energy.

- Frankincense, the Holy Oil, for connection to the Divine
- Sandalwood for prayer
- Vetiver for peacefulness
- Helichrysum for reaching higher dimensions
- Rose for transformation and healing

CLOSING WORDS

My intention for this book was to help shift your view of wealth and abundance. We think that abundance means having the money we desire - but the money is just a nice perk that comes along with our high vibration. True Wealth is feeling abundant in the most amazing moments of our life as well as the challenging moments. Sacred Wealth is being absolutely in love with our life. It's retraining our brain to see the love and beauty in everything. It's looking at our life with awe and amazement because we are so proud of what we've created, no matter what it looks like. Sacred Wealth is about appreciating your life.

It's knowing that you can call in everything you desire with ease, because you already know you have everything you want - it's just about becoming a vibrational match for it and allowing yourself to receive it with grace and appreciation.

How has your view of abundance and wealth shifted after reading this book?

What is the one message that feels most important for you to carry through with you in your life from this point?

What is one of the biggest areas discussed in this book that you feel drawn to continue growing in? (None of this is "one and done" - it's continual balancing and re-aligning).

What support or tools can you utilize to help your continued growth in that area?

Choose an "I AM" statement that can help support your healing in this area and write it down below. Then write it on a Post-It note or somewhere in your phone as a reminder :)

Thank you so much for reading this and giving it your valuable time and energy. I invite you to revisit this book as many times as you'd like so that these healings can occur on another layer. As you know, this work is very much like an onion as we all have many layers of conditioning and programming to shed.

If this book was valuable or supportive to you, please share it in the way that you feel so called, so that we can together spread the message of what abundance truly is. The best way for others to find it is by leaving a review on Amazon (and I would be greatly appreciative of that as well!) Please leave an honest review, as I am always wanting to learn and grow so that I can provide valuable offerings that create deep impact and healing.

As we can create more abundance in the world, we can spread the amount of love that we all experience on a daily basis and that is a beautiful legacy to leave on the world.

Sending you a big hug!

with love
♡ aly Wilkins

PS - All book resources and ways to work with me can be found at my website www.AlyWilkins.Me. You can always reach out at AlyWilkinsAbundance@gmail.com or social media @aly.wilkins on Instagram- I'd love to hear from you!

WORDS ABOUT SACRED WEALTH

"Aly Wilkins is a gifted transformation guide, intuitive healer and leader who serves with high integrity and authenticity. She holds a pristine presence and invites all who are fortunate to work with her and learn from her with an immediately welcoming sense of warmth, acceptance and unconditional love.

Aly's transmission of Sacred Wealth is sure to support many on their paths into awakening infinite abundance while also deeply understanding for themselves what the true meaning of prosperity is and how they can actualize their greatest visions and dreams.

Aly's instruction is rooted in embodiment and energy mastery to such an extent that all who follow her coursework will be truly empowered in becoming their own best healers, leaders and guides. Aly has masterfully outlined a manual in Sacred Wealth for New Earth pioneers and visionaries on how to actualize the most harmonious, thriving world we know we are here to co-create and enjoy. I am honored to know Aly in this lifetime and to have the chance to witness her expansion and contribution to humanity in this most auspicious period of our ascension."

SYDNEY CAMPOS

HOW YOU CAN WORK WITH ALY:

40 Day Sacred Wealth Ritual
A guided 40-day abundance ritual to attract more abundance into your life, utilizing the loving forces of Divinity while simultaneously re-programming your conditioning around abundance. This is a highly rated product and Aly's signature program. Learn more and get access at www.AlyWilkins.Me.

Akashic Record Readings
Visit www.AlyWilkins.Me to book your Akashic Record session with Aly. See the website for reviews and more information.

1:1 Spiritual Mentorship
E-mail AlyWilkinsAbundance@gmail.com to book your mentorship session with Aly. See www.AlyWilkins.Me for reviews and current offerings.

Online Courses, Downloads and Freebies
Visit www.AlyWilkins.Me to shop Aly's Online Store.

Group Retreats + Individual Retreats
See www.AlyWilkins.Me for up-to-date retreat offerings or e-mail AlyWilkinsAbundance@gmail.com if you'd like to book a private or group retreat.

DoTerra Oils
You can purchase DoTerra oils from Aly at www.AlyWilkins.Me to get wholesale pricing.

WORDS ABOUT WORKING WITH ALY

△ *"Aly has been a catalyst for awakening my Soul."*

△ *"I am blown away with the reading. I really loved the experience and the way Aly read the Akashic Records - it felt so authentic and natural. I was completely at ease and grounded."*

△ *"I'm still smiling SO BIG from my session yesterday with Aly. I feel excited and in alignment."*

△ *"My Akashic Record Reading with Aly has completely changed my life."*

△ *"Aly cultivated a very sacred space for our reading and I received the messages that I really needed to hear! Right after our session, I started to notice many synchronicities. The reading has helped direct my energy into alignment."*

△ *"It is really hard to put into words my experience working with Aly. To say the least, it was totally life changing."*

△ *"Aly's ability to hold space is incredible - she'll guide you in a way that feels completely safe in your quantum healing."*

△ *"Aly creates such a magical space for healing and growth that I feel so safe in."*

△ *"A must experience if you want to connect to your higher self . Aly is so supportive and her ability to pick up on what you're not saying is unbelievable. "*

△ *"Aly's reading was a powerful experience that led my soul in new directions. Beyond grateful - Aly is a remarkable human and bright light to the world!"*

△ *"Aly is really just so gifted! I gained so much insight and confirmation from my reading. "*

If you enjoyed this book, please leave a review on Amazon! This is the best way for others to be able to find the book and experience the teachings and learnings within it. Thank you in advance - I am so appreciative for every review.

Made in the USA
Middletown, DE
29 November 2021